TRUCKS, TRUCKING AND YOU

TRUCKS, TRUCKING AND YOU

Hope Irvin Marston
ILLUSTRATED WITH PHOTOGRAPHS

DODD, MEAD & COMPANY, NEW YORK

2 3 4 5 6 7 8 9 10

Library of Congress Cataloging in Publication Data

Marston, Hope Irvin.
    Trucks, trucking and you.

    SUMMARY: Describes different kinds of trucks and
their parts; introduces both female and male truck
drivers; gives advice on trucking careers; relates tales
of heroism by "knights of the road"; discusses CB radio,
driving incentives, and trucking hobbies.
    1. Transportation, Automotive—Freight—Juvenile
literature. 2. Motor-truck driving—Vocational guidance
—Juvenile literature. [1. Trucks. 2. Truck driving.
3. Truck driving—Vocational guidance. 4. Vocational
guidance] I. Title.
HE5613.M37   388.3′24′023   78–7725
ISBN 0–396–07602–5

FOR ARTHUR ══════════════════════════════

PICTURE CREDITS

CONTENTS

1   Introduction   11
2   From Datsuns to Mighty Macks   15
3   What's Under the Hood?   38
4   Who's Behind the Wheel?   60
5   Getting Behind the Wheel of a Big Rig   76
6   Knights of the Road   91
7   The CB Radio and Truckers' Jargon   97
8   Incentives for Good Driving   106
9   Women in Trucking   125
10 Trucking Careers Other than Driving   140
11 Truckers Have Fun   159
12 Trucking Hobbies   164
13 Tomorrow's Trucks   173
    Index   179

TRUCKS, TRUCKING AND YOU

Z-5562-903

UN OIL CO.
OVIDENCE, R.I.

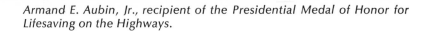
Armand E. Aubin, Jr., recipient of the Presidential Medal of Honor for Lifesaving on the Highways.

1

INTRODUCTION

When Armand E. Aubin, Jr., of Cranston, Rhode Island, climbed into his eighteen-wheeled tanker on the morning of March 9, 1976, he had no idea that he would save another trucker's life before he delivered his 7,900 gallons of gasoline to New London, Connecticut. It was exactly 7:00 a.m. when he fired up his tractor, rolled out of the Sun Oil Company's Providence terminal, and headed south on Interstate 95.

At the same hour twenty-six-year-old Howard Bergman, also operating a tank truck, was heading north on I-95 with a full load of liquid asphalt. At 8:10 a.m. on the outskirts of the village of Hopkinton, an automobile cut in front of him. Bergman's tanker skidded on the shoulder of the road, struck a light pole head-on, and overturned. Within seconds 5,000 gallons of steaming asphalt began forming a deep puddle around his truck. It spilled into the cab of the tractor, trapping the driver.

Moments later Aubin came upon the scene near the Route 3 exit. Never in his thirty-two years of professional trucking had he witnessed such a horrible accident. He brought his rig to a shuddering halt, jumped across the metal guardrail of the median, and waded through the bubbling asphalt, which now measured four inches, in an effort to get to the trapped driver.

He had no time to consider his plastic right hip, inserted surgically just a year earlier, which could have failed him and left him burning in the steaming liquid, too. He knew he must act fast to save the driver. And he did.

"I could hear Bergman screaming, but at first I couldn't see him," Mr. Aubin recalls. "The hot tar cemented my overalls to the tops of my shoes. I guess that's what kept the asphalt from burning my feet. I knew, for both our sakes, I'd better get him out quick."

Howard Bergman was trapped nearly prone in the cab with inches of asphalt already covering his arms and hands. Aubin couldn't see him because of the heavy mist created by the hot liquid. He had only the driver's terrified cries to guide him.

"Please, please, don't turn back," the trapped driver pleaded as he saw his would-be rescuer hopping from one foot to the other and fighting off the intense heat.

Almost faster than it takes to write about it, Aubin climbed atop Bergman's cab, reached in and shut off the engine, then grabbed the scalded driver and pulled him through the popped-out windshield. His prompt action prevented Bergman from being burned to death.

"I kept telling him not to pass out," Aubin says. "I knew I wouldn't be able to lift him if he did."

Fortunately Bergman stayed conscious. Aubin administered first aid to him while another motorist called an ambulance. Within minutes the young driver was enroute to the hospital, badly burned and in shock but, thanks to an heroic fellow trucker, he was alive.

Aubin was concerned about the driver he had rescued. He went often to visit him in the hospital.

"The first time I went, Bergman didn't know who I was," he relates. "His wife asked me if I was the one who had pulled her husband out of the accident. When I said I was, she jumped up and hugged me and cried in my arms. Then she thanked me a million times for saving her husband's life."

One year after the accident, Aubin was presented the Presidential Medal of Honor for Lifesaving on the Highways at a ceremony sponsored by the Rhode Island Truck Owners Association. More than five hundred of Aubin's friends and trucking industry colleagues were on hand for the ceremony. To Aubin, who was also the reigning "Rhode Island Truck Driver of the Year," three faces in the crowd stood out—those of Howard and Marsha Bergman and their six-year-old son who had come again to say "Thank you."

Not every truck driver is called upon to risk his life so dramatically for others as Armand E. Aubin, Jr., did, but you can be sure there are thousands of knights out there, teaming their big rigs, who are as willing and capable of helping in the event of a highway emergency. They're humble but competent, like Aubin, who said, "I am far from being a brave man. I just do what has to be done and then shake after it's all over." This book was written to tell you about these professional drivers and the trucks they drive.

1977 Datsun Li'l Hustler Standard

A mighty Mack Cruise-Liner cab-over-engine tractor pulling a 40-foot van trailer

2

FROM DATSUNS TO MIGHTY MACKS

America's highways are traversed by nearly 30 million trucks. These vehicles range in size and design from the dashing little Datsuns to the big eighteen wheelers like the mighty Mack trucks. Even larger monsters on wheels are used for off-road work such as road building and construction.

Trucks have two basic designs: straight and tractor trailer. Straight trucks are one complete unit, consisting of the cab, the engine, and the body where the cargo is carried. These trucks usually have only two axles: one under the cab and the other at the rear. If the truck is to haul heavy loads, it may have two rear axles. This is called a *tandem*. Straight trucks such as pickups, dump trucks, and wreckers are often smaller and lighter than tractor trailers. But there are also big, heavy straight trucks— cement mixers and garbage trucks, for example.

A Freightliner Conventional Model FLC-12064T

A White Freightliner cab-over-engine

TRACTOR TRAILERS

Tractor trailers are composed of two units. The power-producing unit is called the *tractor*. It has two or three sets of axles with a total of four, six, or ten wheels. Tractors are either conventional or cab-over-engine (COE) in design. Cab-over-engine models have three important advantages over conventionals: they have easy access to the engine for making repairs, greatly improved visibility for the driver, and a roomier driving compartment even in the sleeper models. Some drivers feel wind resistance is less in a conventional. However, the cost is about the same for either model, and wind resistance can be diminished with the addition of an aerodynamic device mounted on the tractor roof.

The load-carrying component of the tractor trailer is called the *trailer*. When the trailer has wheels at the front as well as the back, it is called a *full trailer*. If it has wheels under the back only, it is called a *semi-trailer* or simply a "semi." Semis are connected to the tractor by a heavy, round, hinged plate called a "fifth wheel." A steel kingpin in the trailer floor slips into the

A "fifth wheel," right, enables the trailer to turn freely.

Below: A Budd semi rests on its landing gear.

A double-bottom rig

Triples are seen only in the West where length and weight limitations are more generous.

notch on the fifth wheel and locks it into place. The fifth wheel enables the trailer to turn freely behind the tractor.

An eighteen wheeler is a tractor trailer combination. It may be a semi with eight wheels pulled by a tractor with ten wheels, though the term "eighteen wheeler" is generally used for any tractor trailer combination, regardless of the actual number of wheels.

A semi can be converted to a full trailer by putting a "dolly" under the front end. The dolly is a small platform mounted on wheels. Sometimes it is called a "doodlebug." If a semi must be parked without a tractor, the front end is held up by retractable supports on the trailer which are called the "landing gear."

Some states allow a tractor to pull both a semi and a full trailer. This is called pulling "doubles." In the West where highways run straight for mile after mile, length and weight limitations allow drivers to pull "triple bottoms."

SLEEPERS

Some tractors are sleeper cabs. They have an adjoining bunk area located behind the driver's seat. Other tractors have a sleeper box, a sleeping compartment mounted on the rear of the cab. The sleeper saves the driver the expenses of a motel room.

Sleeper boxes come in several sizes ranging from the 30-inch, skinny, East-Coast 55-foot state special to an 84-inch stand-up, walk-in, Double Eagle mansion. The standard bunk in the industry is 36 inches wide. Obviously, a 30-inch bunk is not the most comfortable, but this size is often a necessity when the sleeper box is added to a conventional cab that will be pulling in a state with a 55-foot tractor-trailer length limitation.

In the mid-1970s, Kenworth introduced its VIT Conventional with a trucker-sized sleeper that has five feet of bedroom and closet area. (VIT means Very Important Truck.) Instead of crawling through a tunnel to get into this sleeper, as you must do on many other models, you simply walk into it from the cab.

The VIT 200 features an aerodynamically designed roof line and a sleeper with bunks, so that both driver and co-driver can sleep at the same time. Twin bunks give both drivers a private

Straight trucks are usually used for short-distance deliveries in both city and country. Pickups are one of the most versatile of all. This 1978 Courier is Ford's addition to the "mini-truck" market.

bed. They can simultaneously log sleep or off-duty time while waiting for a loading dock to open or in any other situation which robs them of valuable legal driving time.

This luxury model has a raised roof which gives 6 feet 10 inches of head room. It is equipped with a portable toilet (chemical) which rolls out of the way when not in use. The sleeper is carefully designed and equipped for the line haul trucker. With such commodious features in his sleeper, the driver truly has a comfortable home on wheels when he teams a VIT 200.

The photographic section starting here shows you the most common kinds of straight trucks and a variety of semis, each designed for a different purpose. You will see late model tractors as well as some off-road vehicles.

Add a camper to your pickup and you can enjoy a comfortable week in the woods with your family.

If you prefer a streamlined appearance, you can get a "chopped" body van and convert it into a mini-motor home.

Vans like this 1973 Chevrolet Step Van 7 are used by dairies, florists, bakeries, and the UPS to make quick deliveries for small loads.

Stake bodies are flatbeds with removable sides. They come in several sizes, and are especially useful to farmers for hauling grain, fertilizer, and livestock. Shown here is a 1972 one-ton stake truck.

Sanitation vehicles like this attractive GMC help keep our cities clean and healthy.

Transit mixers deliver concrete on schedule to those who need it.

An International Paystar 5000 6x4 chassis, mounted with a 5,000-gallon tank, transports raw milk from farm to dairy for a Fort Wayne, Indiana, owner-operator.

White Freightliners (above and below) illustrate two types of dump trucks—the straight body with tandem axle and the dump trailer.

A tow truck is a welcome sight if you have a breakdown.

Fire trucks protect our homes night and day.

Snowplows are important to those who live in the north where snowfall is extremely heavy each winter. Specially designed trucks, such as the Oshkosh, help out the snowbound dweller.

Autocars are tough tractors built by the White Motor Corporation.

Though still an important part of the trucking industry, Brockway trucks have not been manufactured since 1977.

A 1977 Chevrolet Bison

A Crane Carrier Corporation prototype of low-profile, side-packer refuse truck

Diamond Reos are now manufactured by Osterland, Inc., at Harrisburg, Pennsylvania.

Ford Motor Company's over-the-road linehaul diesel truck, the CL-9000, was introduced in the fall of 1977.

FWD heavy-duty construction truck

Freightliner COE, Model FLT-8664T

GMC's 1977 "General," heavy-duty conventional

A custom-built Hendrickson

The New International "S-Series" tandem-axle tractor, Model F-2275

Kenworth "K-Whopper" cab-over-engine model

Mack "Western" R-700 logging tractor

Custom-built Marmon conventional with sleeper and Mark IV air conditioning

Pacific "Roughneck"
P-12-W

Peterbilt "The Working
Class" tractor

The Walter Motor Truck
Company is the largest pro-
ducer of commercial crash
fire rescue vehicles. This
Walter Rapid Intervention
vehicle, below, is used for
airport crash fires.

The White
"Western Star"

Saddle-mounted White Freightliners

The Volvo, though much lighter and smaller
than the other tractors pictured, has proved itself to be efficient, reliable, and durable.

The most common trailer is the box type called a van. Vans haul general freight. Dorsey Trailers markets a van with an AirFlect nose which reduces air drag while increasing cargo space.

A LOOK AT SEMI-TRAILERS

Platform trailers, also called flatbeds, haul bulky, heavy products such as lumber and steel. Trailmobile platform trailers are designed to carry extra-heavy loads.

If products such as food, flowers, or medicine are to be shipped fresh, they will be carried in a refrigerated truck or semi called a "reefer." This Budd reefer is cooled by a Thermo King unit attached to the front of the trailer.

Semi-tankers haul liquid cargo—food products (molasses, milk), chemicals, fuel, cement, and fertilizer. This White Road Boss 2 is a typical tanker.

Livestock semi-trailers have slatted sides. Some have depressed center sections called "possum bellies." The latter type can carry 36 to 40 fat cattle, 90 to 100 feeder calves, or 160 hogs.

When cargo is extremely heavy, tall, or bulky, it must be carried on a lowboy, or gooseneck, semi. Lowboys are very heavy trailers with as many as 22 wheels. Some are pulled by special tractors equipped with a winch and steel cables to help load and unload. They can carry as much as 120,000 pounds. This lowboy is being pulled by a Mack R 700 conventional.

Vehicle carriers bring new automobiles and trucks from the factory to the dealer who sells them to the public.

Logging trucks are designed to carry heavy loads from the forests to the lumber mills. They are flatbeds with strong posts on either side to keep the load from rolling. Autocars are ruggedly built to enable them to carry tremendous weight, as you see here.

OFF-ROAD APPLICATIONS

Some trucks are so heavy they are not permitted to run on our highways. They are used only in off-highway work such as at construction sites. The Mack-Pack shown here is an all-wheel drive, bottom dump that is used in rough terrain.

SLEEPERS

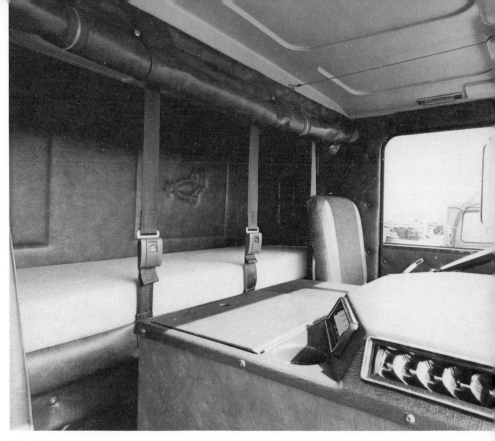

Sleeping quarters in a tractor of necessity must be compact. Shown here is the interior of a Mack Cruise-Liner "short sleeper"—a cab with a two-foot bunk.

Left: Truck manufacturers can add sleeping facilities to their tractors, whether they are conventionals or cab-over-engine models as these GMC tractors, a "General" and an "Astro," illustrate.

3

WHAT'S UNDER THE HOOD?

A driver must know how his truck operates so that he can avoid frequent or long periods of down time. ("Down time" is the time a truck spends in the terminal or repair shop.) He learns how to tell by the sound of his engine if it is operating properly. If his engine doesn't sound right, if it's not performing as it should, or if his instrument readings aren't normal, he assesses the probable cause to see if the problem is something he can fix himself. Should he need to call a service truck, he must request the proper equipment for making the needed repairs.

This chapter is not a complete course in truck mechanics. Its purpose is to give you a general explanation of what makes a truck run.

Trucks have three main parts: the cab, the chassis, and the engine. The cab is the part of the truck where the driver sits. It contains the steering wheel, the seat, and the controls. Some cabs have a sleeper box. The controls in the cab of a small truck may be as simple as those in a car. However, the panel board

LEGEND FOR GAUGES AND INSTRUMENTS

1. Water Temperature Gauge
2. Oil Pressure Gauge
3. Battery — Generating System Gauge
4. Tachometer
5. Speedometer
6. Air Pressure Gauge
7. Air Pressure Gauge
8. Fuel Gauge

9. Right Hand Turn Signal Indicator
10. Brake Air Pressure Indicator
11. Antilock Mounting Indicator
12. Parking Brake Indicator
13. High Beam Indicator
14. Power Divider Lock Indicator
15. Oil Pressure/Water Temperature Indicator
16. Left Hand Turn Signal Indicator

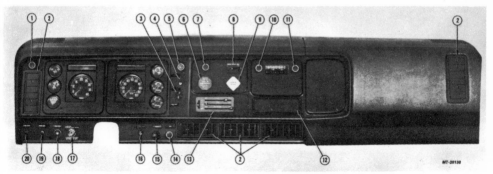

LEGEND FOR CONTROLS

1. Vent Control
2. Heater/Air Conditioning Outlet
3. Wiper/Washer Control
4. Clearance/Identification Light Control
5. Head Light Control
6. Truck-Tractor Protection Valve Control
7. Cigar Lighter
8. Power Divider Lock Control
9. Parking Brake Control
10. Radio Volume Control
11. Radio Tuning Control
12. Ash Receptacle

13. Heater/Air Conditioning Controls
14. Vent Control
15. Throttle Control
16. Engine Stop Control
    Start Assist Control
    Engine Choke Control
17. Ignition Switch
18. Engine Start Control
19. Glow Plug Control
    Fuel Pump Primer Control
20. Ether Start Control
    Fuel Tank Selector Control

The instrument panel of the International S-Series

Some late-model tractors have curved or angled panel boards. Shown here is a Ford cab.

in a large diesel tractor looks as complicated as the cockpit of a DC-7.

The driver of a truck must be able to operate this maze of levers, pedals, switches, gauges, meters, and indicator lights. There may be as many as twelve different things going on at one time which demand his attention. When he is trucking down the freeway pulling 30 tons of valuable freight, he has to be in complete control of his rig.

THE CAB

There are two types of cabs: the conventional (long-nose) and the cab-over-engine (COE). Though their costs are about the same, many drivers have a definite preference.

Conventional supporters feel it is easy to get at their engines

A tilt-hood Ford conventional (above) and an International Transtar
COE (below)

to make repairs, since they have a flip-front fiberglass front end. The driver can stand up on the bumper, give a good yank, and the hood assembly tilts as the shell comes forward over the radiator, giving ready access to the engine.

Conventionals are also favored because they offer a smoother ride. In case of a head-on accident the driver is somewhat protected by the engine. The driver of a conventional has to cope with fewer blind spots because he is closer to the road. Finally, there is decreased wind resistance and that means a more economical run.

Cab-over-engine tractors have several advantages: they are easier to steer in tight spots or small docking areas; they can haul a longer semi-trailer since they have a shorter wheelbase, and that means a greater pay load; some drivers feel they are roomier and offer greatly improved visibility. As one gearjammer put it: "I spend a lot of time in my truck. It's like my house. I don't like being cramped. I started driving in a conventional without a sleeper, and even that seemed crowded. Now I can purchase a conventional with a sleeper, and the driving compartment seems smaller yet. I need a cab-over to be comfortable."

Easy access to the engine is also a selling point for COE tractors. A COE is tilted 45 degrees for normal servicing. It can be tilted 90 degrees if necessary. When you tilt a modern cab, you expose everything. You can get in there and make your repairs and get back on the road where you need to be. In some conventionals you have to tear up the floorboards to make certain repairs. That's time-consuming and therefore costly to the driver.

When a tractor pulls a trailer through the air, it's a little like a submarine sliding through water, except that the sub is built streamlined to slide easily. Trucks aren't so streamlined. When a truck runs into air, the air separates, forming little whirlwinds, called *vortices*, at the cab top, the trailer top, the trailer rear end, and in the gap between the cab and the trailer. The vortices are thrown off the rig at random intervals. This adds greatly to wind resistance. The design of the COE tractor produces greater wind resistance than its counterpart, the conventional, because its lines are much less streamlined.

This GMC conventional is equipped with a roof-mounted Dragfoiler to reduce aerodynamic drag.

The use of top-of-cab wind deflectors substantially reduces wind drag on a tractor trailer. A trailer wind deflector, called a *vortex*, can also be attached to the front of the trailer. It looks like a large fin. It cuts down air turbulence between the tractor and the trailer. The combination of deflectors reduces drag and saves fuel.

A vortex added to the trailer, in addition to the wind deflector, improves fuel economy.

THE CHASSIS

The chassis is the wheeled frame that supports the engine and the cab. In a single-unit truck, it also supports the cargo the truck is carrying. It is made of two strong steel beams fastened together by several cross-pieces. Below the beams the wheels and their axles are connected by springs. The fuel tanks and an air tank for operating the brakes are welded to the framework. Some trucks are built so that extra wheels and axles can be added to the chassis for carrying heavier-than-normal loads.

Tractor trailer combinations have two chassis. The shorter one, called the tractor, supports the cab, engine, and wheels. The longer one, called the trailer, or semi, supports the load-carrying section.

THE ENGINE

The engine is the power unit that turns the wheels of the truck. Modern trucking demands engines that are powerful, economical, and durable. Three kinds of engines are designed to fit the chassis of a truck: gasoline, diesel, and gas turbine. Although the economical diesels are becoming more popular, most small and medium-sized trucks are powered by gasoline. So let's consider the gasoline engine first. Later we will see that it has some similarities with the diesel engine.

THE GASOLINE ENGINE

The job of an engine is to convert the energy of heat into the energy of motion. The conversion begins when the driver puts the key into the ignition lock and turns it. The starter in the ignition activates the cranking motor to start it running. Turning the key opens a path for the electrical current to flow from the battery to the sparkplugs.

Both diesel and gasoline engines operate by means of a charging system (alternator), batteries, and a cranking motor. The battery is the heart of the electrical system. It starts the truck,

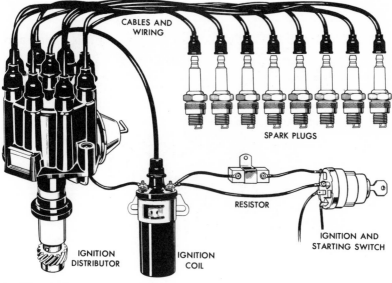

CABLES AND WIRING

SPARK PLUGS

RESISTOR

IGNITION AND STARTING SWITCH

IGNITION DISTRIBUTOR

IGNITION COIL

Ignition system

runs the radio, the heater, the horn, the windshield wipers, and the lights. It is attached to the alternator. The alternator makes electricity from the engine's power when it is running. It sends this electricity back to the battery to replace current that has been used. Older trucks may have a generator and a voltage regulator instead of the single-unit alternator to supply current to the battery.

Some fleets use air starters rather than electrical ones because their owners feel that air starters are more reliable and cheaper to maintain. You can recognize air starters by the sound, a sudden "WHOOOOOEEE." Air starters use a reserve air tank. When the starter is pushed, the air is released into a fan chamber which engages the rest of the mechanism to crank the engine. It works similarly to the electric starter, except it is air driven.

Once the engine is started, the gasoline pump forces gasoline from the tank up through a tube into the carburetor. Vapor from the gasoline is mixed with air in the carburetor. This mixture is

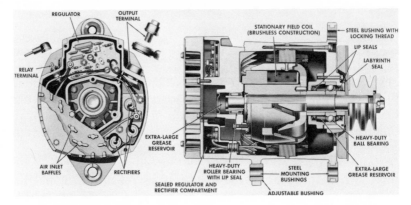

The alternator, the battery, and the cranking motor supply the power to keep a vehicle running. The cutaways show what is inside each of these components.

then forced through an intake valve into the top of each cylinder. Inside the cylinder is a piston which looks like an upside-down tin can sitting on top of a rod.

What takes place inside the cylinders is similar to the action when an old-fashioned muzzle-loading cannon is loaded and fired. There are four stages (cycles) in shooting the cannon: loading, ramming, firing, and cleaning. There are four comparable stages in the operation of the four-cycle gasoline engine. An engine cylinder is loaded with gasoline vapor mixed with

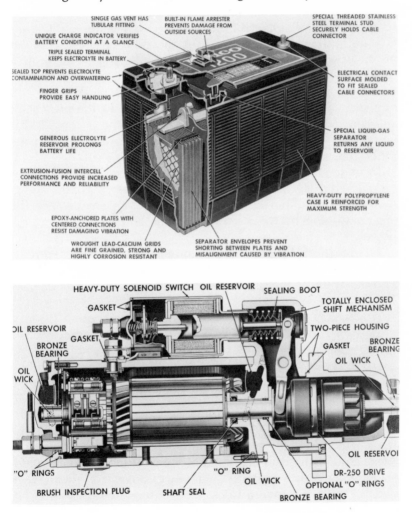

SINGLE GAS VENT HAS TUBULAR FITTING

BUILT-IN FLAME ARRESTER PREVENTS DAMAGE FROM OUTSIDE SOURCES

SPECIAL THREADED STAINLESS STEEL TERMINAL STUD SECURELY HOLDS CABLE CONNECTOR

UNIQUE CHARGE INDICATOR VERIFIES BATTERY CONDITION AT A GLANCE

TRIPLE SEALED TERMINAL KEEPS ELECTROLYTE IN BATTERY

SEALED TOP PREVENTS ELECTROLYTE CONTAMINATION AND OVERWATERING

FINGER GRIPS PROVIDE EASY HANDLING

ELECTRICAL CONTACT SURFACE MOLDED TO FIT SEALED CABLE CONNECTORS

GENEROUS ELECTROLYTE RESERVOIR PROLONGS BATTERY LIFE

SPECIAL LIQUID-GAS SEPARATOR RETURNS ANY LIQUID TO RESERVOIR

EXTRUSION-FUSION INTERCELL CONNECTIONS PROVIDE INCREASED PERFORMANCE AND RELIABILITY

HEAVY-DUTY POLYPROPYLENE CASE IS REINFORCED FOR MAXIMUM STRENGTH

EPOXY-ANCHORED PLATES WITH CENTERED CONNECTIONS RESIST DAMAGING VIBRATION

WROUGHT LEAD-CALCIUM GRIDS ARE FINE GRAINED, STRONG AND HIGHLY CORROSION RESISTANT

SEPARATOR ENVELOPES PREVENT SHORTING BETWEEN PLATES AND MISALIGNMENT CAUSED BY VIBRATION

HEAVY-DUTY SOLENOID SWITCH OIL RESERVOIR SEALING BOOT

GASKET

TOTALLY ENCLOSED SHIFT MECHANISM

OIL RESERVOIR

GASKET

BRONZE BEARING

TWO-PIECE HOUSING

GASKET

BRONZE BEARING

OIL WICK

OIL WICK

"O" RINGS

BRUSH INSPECTION PLUG

SHAFT SEAL

"O" RING

OIL WICK

BRONZE BEARING

OIL RESERVOIR

DR-250 DRIVE

OPTIONAL "O" RINGS

air. This is called the *intake stroke*. The piston inside is comparable to the cannonball, though it does not leave the cylinder. It compresses the gasoline-air mixture in what we call the *compression stroke*.

Above each cylinder is a sparkplug. The sparkplugs are connected to a little round box called the distributor. The distributor sends out electricity to the plugs at the rate of thousands of sparks per minute. Sparks from the plugs ignite the gasoline-air mixture in the cylinder. This causes an explosion that forces the piston downward and turns the crankshaft. This is the *power stroke*.

The crankshaft is made up of a number of cranks forged on one shaft. A connecting rod joins the piston to the crankshaft and converts the up-and-down movement of the piston into rotary movement. When the rods are pushed down, one after the other, they keep pushing the crankshaft around.

To understand this movement think of the foot pedal of your bicycle. Your leg is like the connecting rod as you pedal along. A flywheel mounted on one end of the crankshaft keeps the engine turning between power strokes and smooths out the power.

After each explosion in the cylinder, the piston rises, forcing the burned-up gas out through the exhaust valve at the top of the cylinder and into the pipe called the exhaust. This is the *exhaust stroke*.

Trucks may have four, six, or eight cylinders going through these steps. The firing must take place alternately; otherwise the truck would leap like a jack rabbit and shake itself to bits.

These explosions in the cylinders make the engine very hot. There must be a cooling system to control the heat. The cooling system is one of the most important parts of the engine. Without it the truck would burn itself up.

To cool the engine, the fan draws air through the front of the truck. This cools the water in the radiator. The cooled water flows around the cylinders to cool them. Some drivers have installed fan clutches which save fuel by disengaging the fan when it is not needed. Modern trucks have automatic sensors and fill-

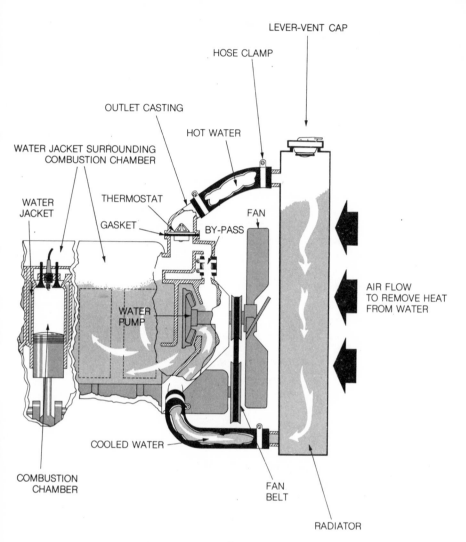

LEVER-VENT CAP

HOSE CLAMP

OUTLET CASTING

HOT WATER

WATER JACKET SURROUNDING
COMBUSTION CHAMBER

WATER
JACKET

THERMOSTAT

GASKET

BY-PASS

FAN

WATER
PUMP

AIR FLOW
TO REMOVE HEAT
FROM WATER

COOLED WATER

COMBUSTION
CHAMBER

FAN
BELT

RADIATOR

How the modern cooling system works

ers to insure that there is always enough water in the radiator.
Some trucks even have a warning system to let you know the
water supply is getting low.

THE DIESEL ENGINE

Diesel engines burn diesel fuel instead of gasoline. They differ from gasoline engines in that they have no carburetor or spark-plugs. Instead, the diesel fuel is injected directly into the cylinders rather than being mixed with air before it enters them.

As in gasoline engines, each cylinder has two valves. The air intake valve is like the door of a stove which you open when you want to put in more wood. The exhaust valve is like the chimney which allows the smoke (burned gases) to escape when the damper is open. As with gasoline engines, this procedure occurs in four cycles.

The diesel oil is squirted (injected) into the cylinder by a very high-powered fuel injection pump. The fuel explodes in the

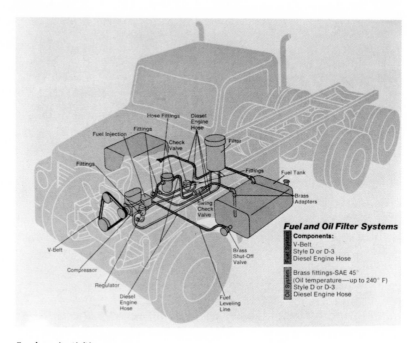

Fuel and oil filter systems

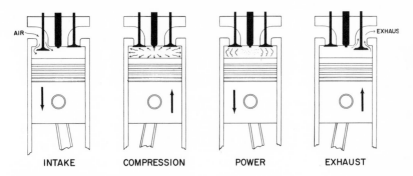

AIR			→ EXHAUST
INTAKE	COMPRESSION	POWER	EXHAUST

Four-cycle diesel engine

hot compressed air. The piston is driven downward. As it goes down, it turns the crankshaft. The revolutions of the crankshaft are measured by rpm's (revolutions per minute). In most diesel trucks the cycle is governed to repeat itself 2,150 times per minute, and some even more than that. This sounds fast, but it isn't. There are racing car engines which operate at more than 10,000 rpm's.

DIESEL VS. GASOLINE ENGINES

The real advantage in owning a gasoline-powered truck is in cost—cost of replacement. You can replace the whole engine for a fraction of what it would cost to replace a diesel engine.

Today's gasoline engines may run more than 200,000 miles before they need to be overhauled or replaced. However, they have less power and they can't go as fast as diesels. The 55 mph limit doesn't hurt the drivers of gasoline rigs so much, since they don't have sufficient power to pull faster than that.

Diesel engines cost more because they must have heavier gears and shafts. Since the imposition of the "double nickles"— the 55 mph limit—engines have been redesigned to get maximum torque at lower rpm's, and manufacturers have begun to gear the diesels differently. These new "fuel squeezers" have a different rear end ratio that allows them to operate economically

Major tractor manufacturers produce both gasoline- and diesel-powered vehicles. Shown here are two 1977 Chevrolets. The Series 70 gasoline model is on the left. You can recognize the Series 90 diesel tractor on the right by its smokestacks.

at the slower engine speeds and still have built-in power to top the hills.

Diesel truckers insist that their engines have advantages which outweigh the higher initial costs. First of all, diesel engines are efficient. They get more power per unit of fuel burned than any other engine available for automotive use. Diesel fuel is cheaper than gasoline and it is safer to use because it's much less flammable. Diesel rigs produce less pollution than the family car; they deliver sustained economy in service; and they require fewer repairs in comparison with gasoline engines.

Diesel engines run best at steady speeds for long periods of time. That's why they are preferred for heavy-duty, long-distance hauling.

When you purchase a new truck, you can specify whether you want diesel or gasoline power. If you can afford it, you'll save money in the long run with the diesel engine.

THE GAS TURBINE ENGINE

The gas turbine engine is really a jet engine. Its burning, expanding gases press against the blades of a rotor, spinning it and its shaft. The whirling shaft turns the reduction gears. This reduces the speed but increases the power of the shaft going to the transmission.

Gas turbines can burn low-cost fuels such as kerosene, liquified petroleum, or cheap jet fuel, but their fuel consumption is tremendous. They cause less air pollution and they are much lighter than the heavy diesel engines. They are extremely long-lasting. They can be removed from a worn-out truck chassis and installed in a new truck. They well may be the engines of the future. Right now they are too expensive.

GETTING POWER TO THE WHEELS—THE DRIVE TRAIN

Once the engine is running, its power must be transmitted to the drive train. The drive train is made up of the parts of the truck through which this power is channeled to the wheels. It consists of the clutch, the transmission (gearbox), the drive shaft, and the rear-axle assembly (rear end).

The power is carried to the wheels in a carefully designed manner. It would waste both time and fuel if the driver had to turn off the engine each time he wanted to stop his truck. The clutch provides the means for disconnecting and reconnecting the engine to the drive train without turning it off. Pressure and friction make the clutch work. When the two parts of the clutch press together, the crankshaft makes the transmission shaft turn.

The drive shaft is a long, round, metal rod that transmits power from the transmission main shaft to the final drive in the rear axle. The axle is the rod that runs between the wheels. This axle has to turn round and round to make the wheels turn. But the drive shaft does not run in the same direction as the axle. Instead, the two are joined at right angles in the shape of a T lying flat. Power coming through the drive shaft has to be distributed evenly as it turns to the right and to the left to get to the wheels. This is accomplished by a group of gears called the differential. The differential is located where the drive shaft meets the rear axle.

GEARS

Gears are metal wheels with teeth around their outer edges. The teeth of one gear fit into the teeth of another as both are turned. You can see how this works if you place the fingers of your right hand between the fingers of your left hand. Then turn your right hand. The left hand turns with it. Right? One hand turns the other. It is the same with gears. One gear turns the other.

You will find different kinds and sizes of gears in a gearbox. Some mesh their edges as they run side by side. Others operate like a hand-operated egg beater. The edge of one gear meets a second gear in a T formation. One turn of the larger gear on the beater turns the smaller one several times. It multiplies the power as it turns. Likewise, the gears in a transmission multiply the turning power, called torque, from the engine.

Heavy-duty trucks may have as many as twenty gears. The average company-owned truck has ten. The modern "fuel squeezer," the high-rise torque engine, has five to ten speeds.

The gears in the transmission are controlled by the gearshift in the cab. The gearshift makes the wheels turn at different speeds while the engine is running at a fairly constant rate. If you have pedaled a bicycle, you can understand why different gears are necessary. When you want to get started on your bike, you have to pedal harder than you pedal after you get moving. The low gears on a truck are used to get a heavy load moving, or to pull it up a steep grade. High gears are used on the open highways where more speed and less power are required.

Heavy trucks may use a double differential called a "tandem"

If you look carefully at the cutaway (below) of this Spicer 50 Series
transmission, you can see various types of gears.

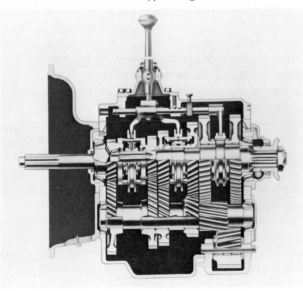

or "twin-screw." The differentials are connected by a short drive shaft. A power divider transmits torque evenly to both wheels. A Mack power divider is similar to "limited slip differential" in a car. A 3 percent slippage on one wheel automatically throws the power to the opposite side. There is another type of divider that can be locked in or out whenever the driver chooses to do so. This is called "direct drive." It is a bit tricky learning when to touch the brakes in the automatic device. The locked divider is preferred if your travels are through muddy highways.

AUTOMATIC VS. MANUAL TRANSMISSION

Truck drivers can choose between two basic transmissions: automatic and manual. The majority of drivers choose the manual because it gives finer control. All manual transmissions include a mechanical clutch. Eventually the clutch must be repaired or replaced. That's a costly repair. The trucker is losing money while he's down waiting for it to be fixed.

There are several advantages to the automatic transmission. Trip time is reduced through positive shifts at the most efficient time for shifting. Some drivers consider automatics safer to operate since the driver can keep both hands on the wheel all the time. They are easy to learn to drive if the new driver has driven a passenger car that's automatic. They reduce down time since there are no periodic clutch problems. They give better overall performance because the engine power is matched to performance requirements. And they are easier on the driver.

On the negative side are two disadvantages: they do use more fuel than the manual transmission and they cost about three times as much.

Trucks used for extremely heavy work, as in construction or in off-road applications, use automatic transmissions. However, because of the cost and the fuel consumption, most long-distance haulers stick to manual transmissions. One independent driver summed up his feelings about transmissions this way: "I'm ready for an automatic myself. If I were to buy a new truck and could afford it, I would get an automatic. It's easier on the truck, on the drive line, and it's easier on the driver!"

THE BRAKING SYSTEM

Because trucks differ in size, payload, and purpose, they also differ in braking systems. Small trucks generally have a hydraulic system of drum, disc, or power brakes. Drum brakes are usable on all wheels. A brake drum is a hollow metal cylinder attached to each wheel. Two brake shoes are usually fitted inside each wheel where they are fastened to a hydraulic wheel cylinder. Each shoe has a lining. When the driver steps on the brake pedal, the linings are forced against the inner surface of the brake drum. This converts the energy of motion to the energy which is lost in the air, causing the truck to slow down.

Some trucks have disc brakes on the front wheels. These brakes do not have drums or shoes. Instead, a metal disc rotates with the wheel and lined calipers replace the shoes. When the brakes are applied, the caliper pushes a pad against the disc. This action is similar to bicycle hand brakes which are really blocks that rub against both sides of the wheels.

Both large and small trucks can be equipped with power brakes. They make braking easier because they multiply the pressure exerted on the foot pedal.

AIR BRAKES

The big SWOOOSH you hear at stop signs or red lights as the giant rigs prepare to move out is caused by air being released from the air brakes. Tractor trailers and other large trucks are equipped with air brakes because this type offers the greatest efficiency in stopping when the cargo and equipment are heavy.

In tractors equipped with air brakes, compressed air goes through pipes or hoses to a control valve. The valve responds to pressure changes. It adjusts pressure which sets or releases the brakes. This is done by applying a force in the brake chamber located between the brake shoe and the wheel. Each wheel has its own brake chamber and two air reservoirs. One reservoir is for regular use, the other is for emergencies. Whenever the pressure in the air line drops to 60 pounds, the reservoir pressure activates the brake cylinder. This forces the shoe against the

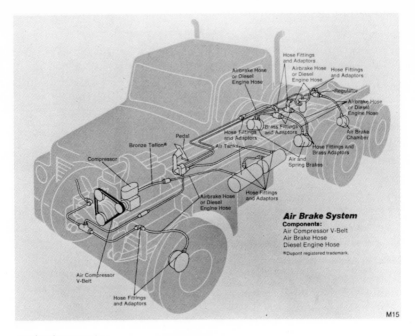

Air-brake system

wheel—an important safety feature. Should the trailer break loose from the tractor, or should there be a leak in the air line, the air brakes will be activated, bringing the trailer to a halt.

It takes skill to apply air brakes. If the driver is not careful, he can lock the wheels. Or skid the rig and tear the tires. If he turns too sharply while braking, the trailer may keep going forward faster than the tractor. That can swing the rig into a jackknife and out of control.

ENGINE RETARDERS

Many heavy trucks are equipped with some sort of engine brake called a retarder. Engine brakes are important for controlling truck speed downhill with a very heavy cargo or in stop-and-go traffic. They reduce driving time in hilly terrain by permitting the truck to descend at a faster but still safe speed. They also trim maintenance costs on the service brakes. They extend the life of the tires, the regular brake linings, and the drums. They can be used effectively on icy pavements.

One of the most popular engine retarders is called the Jake Brake. It is manufactured by the Jacobs Manufacturing Company which also markets an electric retarder called the Jake"er". The Jake"er" can be used on gasoline or diesel engines. In fact, it may be used on any vehicle that has a drive shaft.

Engine brakes manufactured by other companies are sold by the trade names BrakeSaver, the Blue Ox, and the Dynatard.

121 BRAKES

In the mid-1970s, the Department of Transportation of the federal government passed a law called the Federal Motor Vehicle Safety Standard 121. This regulation establishes performance standards for stopping in a certain distance with a certain load, without swerving out of a twelve-foot lane. The manufacturer can install any kind of equipment he wants—as long as it meets this performance standard. The equipment designed to meet these standards has been designated "121 brakes." They are an anti-lock braking system. They have been constructed to prevent jackknifing in those situations where a jackknife is caused by wheel lock-up. Like any new product, there are problems with these brakes. If these problems can be solved, 121 brakes could become a valuable safety feature that no trucker would want to be without.

4

WHO'S BEHIND THE WHEEL?

Truck drivers differ as much as the trucks they drive. So do their jobs. Some of them, like firemen and repairmen, drive trucks as part of some other job. One kind of driver takes his company's truck over a fairly short, regular route each working day. He delivers such products as milk, bread, or mail. Often he has duties besides driving. He must sell, collect, or perform some specific type of service for his customers. This driver is important as he scoots from customer to customer in his little four-wheeler.

Another group of drivers works for trucking companies. These operators drive larger, heavier, more complicated trucks. Many pull eighteen-wheeled combination tractor trailer rigs, called "eighteen wheelers." Each day they deliver thousands of dollars' worth of cargo to waiting customers.

In this chapter you will meet five drivers. Each differs from the others in what he drives, where he goes, and what he hauls. Perhaps as you read about these men, you'll decide what kind of truck driver you'd like to become.

NORMAN WESTCOTT: BREAD TRUCK DRIVER

Morning comes early for Norman Westcott. He leaves his home at 4:30 a.m. and heads for the Millbrook Bread terminal a few miles away. He must pick up the company truck he usually drives and load it with the freshly baked goods that arrive in the night from the company's bakery in Syracuse.

As Norm loads his truck, he keeps things in order. Who wants to move twelve shelves of fresh bread to get at the doughnuts at each stop? His more than thirty-five years of experience with this company have taught him to load carefully and efficiently.

He is soon making his rounds to the Watertown restaurants, delivering fresh bread, rolls, and doughnuts for the early breakfast customers. By the time he has finished servicing the restaurants, he is ready for his own breakfast. He relaxes momentarily over his morning coffee and then hustles on to the other delivery points around the city. By the time he arrives at the supermarkets

Fresh bakery products are delivered daily by thousands of truck drivers.

and the little stores, they will be open and ready to receive their fresh baked goods to sell to their customers that day.

Millbrook buyers do not usually order ahead. Norm has learned through the years how much of each product will probably be required at each stop. When he arrives, he fills his basket with what he thinks the customer will want that day. He makes the delivery, checks the customer's request, leaves what is needed, and picks up anything that did not sell yesterday. (State laws prohibit baked goods from staying on the shelves day after day.) He presents the bill to his customer, receives payment, and then hastens on.

Norm must keep moving. The first ten years that he worked for this company, he had an out-of-town route. He drove many miles between stops, but there were fewer of them. Now he has much less driving, but the stops are time-consuming as he makes his deliveries and exchanges pleasantries with each buyer.

Norm is paid a salary and a commission. The more goods he sells his customers, the greater the commission he will receive. He watches for new markets opening within his designated territory. He visits them, offering samples of his baked goods. It is to his advantage to take on a new customer.

Once he has finished his route, Norm heads back to the terminal. He refuels his truck enroute and makes a note if there is any problem with it. The next morning he will be driving the same one. If something needs repaired or checked he must call it to the attention of the company's mechanic. Should there be a major problem with the truck, he will be given the spare truck to drive until his is repaired.

His work is not done when he backs his truck into the company garage. Now he must settle up his finances. Each driver must account for all of the goods he left with. He must return it or have enough money to cover its cost. He may also return some day-old goods which his customers did not sell. He will have given the customer credit for this. Now he must be sure his books balance. Once he has tended to these accounting details, Norm's working day is through. It has been a long one. It will be six or seven o'clock before he arrives home to the hearty, hungry man's dinner his wife Eunice has waiting for him.

Gregg Irvin teams his father's tri-axle dump truck.

GREGG IRVIN: COAL HAULER

Nineteen-year-old Gregg Irvin has been driving his father's tri-axle dump truck for three years. Gregg hauls coal from the strip mines to the tipples where it is washed and crushed. He has a long working day, but he doesn't mind, since he gets paid a percentage of what his truck earns.

"I like to be first in line when the mine opens," he says. "That way I can get home earlier or maybe pick up an extra load. I leave home between 4:30 and 5:00 each morning, depending on how far it is to the mine where I'll be hauling from that day. If I get home by four, I consider that early."

Sometime during the evening the company to whom Gregg's truck is leased calls to tell him where he should work the following day. "I don't know where I'll be next Wednesday," Gregg says, "but I have a pretty good idea where I am going tomorrow unless we are finishing up one job and are ready to be dispatched to a different mine."

Gregg likes trucking 24 tons of coal from mine to tripple. "I meet a lot of nice people," he says, "—the other drivers, the

Gregg hauls coal from the strip mines of central Pennsylvania to the tipples.

Changing a flat is part of the long day's work for Gregg.

weighmasters, the loaders. I get to see lots of country, too. There's always something interesting. On my first run this morning I saw a herd of deer."

Gregg refuels his truck on his way home each afternoon. He kicks the tires to see if one is flat, as he has done several times during the day. "You have to thump them to tell if one is flat," he says. "You can't tell just by looking at them if one of them is flat. The duals hold each other up." Duals are a pair of wheels and tires mounted together on the same side of one axle.

The young blond driver takes good care of his father's Mack truck. "If anything goes wrong with my truck during the day, I try to fix it myself that night. I can fix a lot of things," he explains. "I learned to do that by hanging around the garage when our trucks were being repaired. When we're paying $14 per hour for labor, we stick around to make sure no one is goofing off. I watch pretty closely and that's how I learn. When my dad had hired drivers, I took their trucks in for repairs. I learned a lot from watching the mechanics at work on our own vehicles."

"Badfinger" is Gregg's CB handle. When asked about the CB radio in his cab, he had these comments. "I could live without it, but it's a big help. We have a lot of narrow roads where there's only room for one truck. The CB contact saves us from having to do a lot of backing."

Gregg has this advice for anyone who wants to become a truck driver. "Find someone who drives and who will let you ride with him. Have him teach you the technical things like downshifting on a grade, starting and stopping, turning around, and backing. Keep your eyes open, ask questions, and pay attention to everything!"

JOHN AUCTER: FROM GLUER TO GEARJAMMER

John Aucter worked for Climax Manufacturing Company in Castorland, New York, a number of years before he was given the opportunity to become an over-the-road driver delivering the company's paper products to several major cities in the East.

"I started out with Climax as a gluer, putting boxes together.

Before he became a driver, John Aucter worked at various jobs necessary for the manufacturing of his company's products.

Then I became a packer preparing the boxes for shipment. Next I was a materials handler, working out on the loading docks.

"I had been with Climax about five years when the company needed another driver. The traffic manager asked me if I were interested. I said I was. I got my permit and they put me to work out in the yard getting used to handling the big rigs. Two weeks later I made my first solo trip to New York. That was twelve years ago."

John, who is known as "Sodbuster" to his CB friends, teams a beautiful blue and white GMC Astro tractor trailer. It belongs to Climax, but he has full responsibility for it. No one else drives his tractor. "It's better to drive for the company in their truck," he says. "If something happens to the truck, it's up to me to get it fixed, but it's not my expense. I treat it as though it were my own, but I don't have the expenses of this rig's upkeep. Since I always drive the same thing, I can keep my bedroll and other personal belongings in it."

John's work week begins Sunday afternoon. He says, "I leave early enough Sunday afternoon to get to my first delivery point around midnight. That allows me time to get my eight hours off the road before I make the next day's deliveries and pick ups and head home again. I have to have enough time to drive back home before I've used up ten hours of driving time. Federal regulations allow only ten hours of consecutive driving. Then I must be off duty for eight hours before I may drive again.

"I haul to Boston, Providence, or New York. Because of the distances to these cities from my home, I am home only an hour or so each day, usually about dinner time. Saturday night is the only night I sleep at home unless I don't have to go back out. If there's no load to be delivered or if I choose not to work, then I'll spend the night at home. I am limited to seventy hours of driving time a week by the ICC regulations. My time is recorded in my log book.

"When business is slow, each of us drivers makes fewer trips a week. The loads are divided among us. The dispatching is done on a wheel based on seniority. I'm number five. When there is goods to be delivered, the top man gets the first load. It runs down through the numbers. If there are only six loads, the seventh man doesn't get to go out that day.

"After we have delivered our company's paper boxes, we pick up a return load of scrap paper. Sometimes we must help load this scrap. It depends on the unionization at the terminal. We may have to go to another city to get the scrap paper. If we have to come back empty, it's not money out of our pockets. We have an advantage over the owner operators who get paid by gross weight. Hauling 'post holes' doesn't hurt us."

John is sympathetic toward those who want to drive today, but who lack experience. "It's tough breaking in," he agrees. "Most companies want experienced drivers only. I was lucky the way I got started. It doesn't usually happen that way."

He offers these suggestions to would-be truckers. "Keep your ears open. Listen in any time you hear some one talking about trucks. Keep looking. Eventually you'll find someone who'll give you a chance to learn to drive."

ROLAND IRVIN: LONG-DISTANCE HAULER

Trucks do not earn money for their owners while they are sitting idle or empty. That's why trucking companies have devised a number of relay systems to keep their rigs moving. In one type of relay, different truckers drive the same rig toward an ultimate destination. In another type, a trucker runs to an agreed switching point. He exchanges rigs with another driver from his company. Then he returns to his original terminal or departure point with the second truck. Meanwhile the second driver returns to his terminal with the first man's rig. This system allows each driver to run his allotted road time. The freight is delivered on schedule, and each driver has had the advantage of covering a route he knows well.

The C. R. England and Sons trucking company for whom Roland Irvin drives has a different relay system, but one that gives the drivers the advantage of driving routes with which they have developed a familiarity. Rollie's route begins at a truck stop in Milesburg, Pennsylvania, about fifteen minutes from his home, and ends at Providence, Rhode Island. Actually the goods he is carrying for his company was picked up by another driver in Greenville, Ohio, and brought by him to Milesburg.

At Milesburg, Rollie and the other driver switch trailers; Rollie heads towards Providence and the second driver retraces his route to Greenville. The company terms this procedure "turning around." To get "turned" means to retrace your route with another driver's trailer instead of taking your initial load to its final destination.

The company's dispatcher knows if a shipment must be rushed and whether the driver will have time to get it there before he uses up his ten hours of driving time. If he can't make it, then another driver will be sent to meet him at a prearranged point and turn him. The two will switch "boxes," but not tractors, and head in the direction from which they have come.

Rollie's route allows him to be home every other day. He takes the company tractor, a shining 74 Kenworth, home with him. As with the Climax drivers, he can treat that truck as

A company driver arrives at Milesburg to swap trailers with Rollie Irvin who will carry the cargo to Rhode Island.

though it were his own. No one else drives it.

"I have it set up the way I want it now," he says. "I've got some extra 'goodies' on it for my own comfort. My high back seat is one of them. It gives me added support when I'm running down the interstates. Also I have chrome rims on my drive axles, and I have an airfoil.

"The company lets us personalize our trucks. Right now mine is being painted. When it comes back from the shop, I should be able to run it for another three years. It has about 800,000 miles on it now. It's got a good engine, a 350 Cummins, and a ten-speed Road Ranger transmission. I put about 5,000 miles on it a week, so I appreciate its power."

Headquarters for the C. R. England company is in Salt Lake City. The general pattern for the company drivers is to receive a call from the dispatcher telling them there are loads ready. The drivers report to the dispatcher who hands them an envelope labeled with their names, the numbers of the tractors and trailers

Rollie takes time to catch up on his log book.

they will be driving, and their destinations. Inside the envelopes are the waybills, delivery times, and addresses where the goods are to be carried.

Before starting out, each driver inspects his tractor and trailer carefully and certifies on the back of his log sheet that everything is in satisfactory order. Then he records his time and hits the road. He may be hauling fresh produce, swinging beef (sides of slaughtered beef hanging from racks), lamb, fresh oysters, clams, or some other product.

If there are co-drivers, the two will carry the load from its source to its destination on the East Coast. If the driver is traveling alone and has lots of time, he can also make the entire trip without getting turned. Then he will pick up a shipment and head west. Drivers who operate on this kind of schedule may be on the road for six weeks at a time.

Rollie prefers running without a co-driver. "The only time I have a co-driver is when I get behind. Normally I don't take another driver with me because I can't get used to sleeping behind someone else. If I had the same person with me all of the time, I suppose I could get used to his driving. But I don't. It's hard to sleep while your rig is moving. When I do run with someone, it's only for a couple of days. After two days we're both so tired we fall asleep in the bunk with little trouble."

Sometimes Rollie has to help load or unload his trailer. If the load must be "fingerprinted"—that is, loaded by hand without using a forklift or rollers, he has to do it himself. Fragile glass items, delicate instruments, or very perishable fresh produce have to be fingerprinted. Usually his company will provide a man to help him. "Some businesses won't let me unload myself," he says with disgust. "They charge me to let them unload my cargo. Of course my company has to pay that ridiculous charge."

Rollie gets paid by the mile and by the number of drops (stops to unload cargo) he makes. "Trucking is really a great job," he says. "I like it a lot. I plan to team that big ol' K-Whopper for a long time to come."

RAY BYLER: OWNER-OPERATOR

The menacing chrome bulldog stood guard over the hood of Ray Byler's big blue F 700 Mack. He had kept his vigil in the backyard since Thursday evening when Ray returned home.

Early Sunday morning the Mason and Dixon agent called Ray. "Do you want to haul a load of steel from Reading to Fort Wayne?" he asked. He told him the weight and the specific deliv-

Ray Byler swings into his cab to check his gauges prior to his trip.

ery point. Ray was interested. It would be a good load to pull. He would earn 75 percent of the shipping charge for carrying it. That wouldn't be a bad load at all. He'd make about $500 on it. "Pick up at the Dana Corporation at five this afternoon," the agent said.

About 4:15 Ray said goodbye to his family. He went to his agent's terminal to pick up his manifest and his advance check. He checked in with the guard forty-five minutes later at Dana. The guard told him where he was to get loaded. Ray backed his rig into the bay (dock) and supervised the loading. Then he put the chains around the steel to keep it from shifting. He double-checked to make sure the kingpin on the fifth wheel had been latched. Then he swung his limber six-foot frame into the familiar cab.

He turned the key in the ignition, tramped the pedal, and smiled as the engine turned over and caught on the first try. He set his parking brake. Leaving the engine running, he picked up his pre-trip checklist and began to note each item. There were many things to be checked for safety's sake and to comply with the regulations of the Interstate Commerce Commission. Oil and air pressure. Low air warning signal. Instrument panel. Horn. Windshield wipers and washer. Heater-defroster. He checked his mirrors and adjusted the left one a bit. He made sure he had his fire extinguisher, flares, extra fuses, and red flags. He hoped he'd not have to use these things, but they were ready if he needed them. Next he turned on all lights, set the emergency trailer brake, and hopped out.

Circling his eighteen wheeler, he made certain all of his lights were working. That included headlights, sidemarkers, turning signals, 4-way flashers, taillights, and reflectors. He inspected his tires and his Dayton wheel lugs. He checked out the load binders again, the chains he had put around his cargo. He made certain the fuel tanks and their caps were okay. Finally he checked the "glad hands" (air hoses), the electrical plug, and the fifth wheel latch that joined his flatbed trailer to the mighty Mack tractor. Everything was in order outside.

Ray returned to the cab and shut down the engine. He released the trailer emergency brake, applied the service brakes, and noted the air loss. All signals were "Go" inside as well. He fastened his seat belt and reached for his log book to record his starting time.

His bookkeeping details completed, he pushed the accelerator, started his engine, and listened as the mighty diesel burped,

A pre-trip inspection is made both inside and outside the rig.

caught, and filled the cab with a "rarin'-to-go" roar. Then the Pennsylvania double-clutcher reached for his gearshift. He knew the numbers and his shifts were forceful and smooth as he moved out. He worked his way up through the gears as he headed toward the Warren Street Bypass that led to Route 183 North.

About twenty miles down the road, he stopped at the truck stop to refuel. Because it saved both time and money, Ray usually pulled into the self-service lane. A few cents savings per gallon added up when you were refueling a thirsty tractor trailer.

His tanks topped, he took his advance check into the truck stop, cashed it, paid for his fuel, and returned to his rig. The money left over would be used for turnpike fees, eating, and other travel costs.

Shortly thereafter the "Bulldogger" pulled onto the bustling superslab. He keyed his CB mike. "Breaker, one nine. How about ya', Eastbound? How are we lookin' over your shoulder?"

"No bears around! Put the hammer down!" was the immediate comeback.

"Thanks, Good Buddy. Have a safe trip yourself. Three's. Catch yuh later. The Bulldogger. We westbound and down!"

Ray settled into a more comfortable position. He checked his speedometer as well as the other gauges. He would be careful to keep his heavy load under control and within the 55 mph limit. He had a long ride ahead. When he got to Fort Wayne, he would back into the dock, take the chains off, and stay with his truck while it was being unloaded. Then he'd head for the nearest phone to call the Mason and Dixon central office in Kingsport, Tennessee, to see where he was likely to find a return load. He knew he'd have to go to Cleveland or to Indianapolis to get it.

He thought about his wife Joanne and his four kids—his little truckers—that he had left behind. He'd miss them. This load would keep him away from home for at least three days . . . maybe four . . . if he had to wait around for a return load. That was one of the disadvantages for the owner-operator who leased his truck. Yet he liked working for Mason and Dixon. He would rather be driving his powerful Mack for them than to be driving a truck that belonged to someone else. He was fiercely proud of his rig, and like many owner-operators, he kept it in good shape with its chrome "a-shining."

Ray Byler's interest in trucking can be traced to his father who was also an over-the-road driver. When he first became interested in driving, it was easier to get started than it is today. Recognizing that fact, Ray offers this advice to you who want to drive the big rigs some day. "Drive anything for two years, even if it doesn't bend in the middle [a reference to a tractor trailer combination]. You'll get exposed to traffic and a variety of driving conditions and that's what experience is all about."

5

GETTING BEHIND THE WHEEL OF A BIG RIG

If you wish to become a truck driver, you can begin your preparation in high school. By all means take driver education. If you can, get into a class in bookkeeping or general business. Take typing if it's available. Most important, if you can take a course in a vocational or technical school, enroll in auto mechanics.

But don't expect to hop behind the wheel of a semi the moment you are graduated. It takes skill to manage an eighteen wheeler. Besides, the United States Department of Transportation has laid down some minimum qualifications for long-distance drivers engaged in interstate commerce.

First of all, you must be twenty-one years old. Don't despair. That means you have three years to prepare yourself. The truth of the matter is you probably have a longer time than that. Because of the costly insurance rates, many firms will not hire drivers under twenty-five.

Rich "Corncob" Muthler is happiest when he's behind the wheel of his tri-axle Mack dump truck.

What do you do while you are waiting to grow older? You get a job around trucks. In a garage. At a truck stop. At a freight-loading dock. Or with a small moving company. It doesn't really matter where you begin, so long as you work hard, learn how to do your job well, and keep your ears open.

If you can get a job with a common carrier, a private fleet, or

His job today is to get this Westbound "pumpkin" (its nickname be-cause of its color) refueled. Tomorrow he may be teaming it.

a leasing company, take it. These companies have departments concerned with many phases of trucking. They can teach you about operations, sales, safety, purchasing, and maintenance. It's important to gain experience in each of these areas, especially if you aim to own your own big "Pete" (a Peterbilt truck) someday.

Open Road, a popular magazine with truckers, suggests a job with a freight company as the best place to learn to drive—especially if you can get the yard "wrangler's" or yard "hostler's" job. The wrangler picks up trailers in the freight yard and spots them into the dock to be loaded or unloaded. Then he pulls them away and drops them in the yard. You can gain a great deal of driving experience in this manner.

Many truck drivers get their start as pump jockeys or "grease monkeys" at a truck stop. Quite often the "lube men" are the ones who drive the big rigs on and off the grease pits or wash racks. Either of these jobs puts you in position to make friends with the drivers and gives you good experience in driving, even though the distances are short. By and by you may find a driver who is willing to take you with him and "show you the ropes."

When you are looking for a job, it's wise to contact moving companies or local dispatchers. Tell them you are interested in becoming a driver's helper—that you would like to become a driver eventually.

More than one big rig operator learned how to care for his truck while working at a truck stop, servicing a variety of makes and models.

Make yourself available to help owner-operators load and unload. It's hard work, but the pay isn't bad. Who knows? When the driver sees how determined you really are, he may invite you to be his helper on his next run. You can advertise on bulletin boards in truck stops and at truckers' motels that you are available for loading and unloading help.

So far we have talked about actual work experience around trucks. While you are getting that, you would be wise to pick up some business courses at night school. Bookkeeping, accounting, and business law are courses you should take.

Time marches on. You have now reached your twenty-first birthday. You have worked three years in a couple of trucking jobs and you've had a little experience jockeying the big rigs around the yard. Now consider enrolling in a truck driver's school. Most of these schools are not too expensive. They may last from a few months to a year.

Choose your trucking school carefully. Some excel in taking your money without teaching you very much that you need to know. Unfortunately there is no official accrediting agency devoted solely to trucking schools. The Bureau of Motor Carrier Safety began a study in 1976 that will eventually lead to a set of standards. However, it will take at least four years for the results of the research to be validated.

Ask your state education department or vocational education commissioner where you can get trucking training. The National Association of Trade and Technical Schools, 2021 L Street NW, Washington, D.C. 20036, publishes an annual directory of accredited vocational schools. You will find some reputable trucking schools listed there. Many would-be drivers have taken training at a trucking school and then have not been able to get a job driving. For that reason, they "bad mouth" trucking schools. It is true that there are flim-flam artists in this field. That's why you are advised to check the school out carefully before enrolling. Talk with its graduates. See if they are satisfied. Find out if the school delivered all that it had promised. Visit the training facilities. See if they are up-to-date. Find out how much classroom instruction is offered. Ask to see the credentials of the in-

Instructor Tom Johnstone (left) watches as students Larry Donalds, Roseville, Minnesota, (top) and Rick Gottwaldt, Linolakes, Minnesota, install Transtar F-4370 glider kit on a rebuilt chassis as a 916 Area Vocational Technical Institute's project for "Truck Week '76."

structors. See how much actual driving time you will have.

If you live in Minnesota, consider the 916 Area Vocational Technical Institute in White Bear Lake. This school offers excellent training in truck mechanics and in truck driver training. Visitors to "Truck Week '76," a national truckers' exposition held in Chicago, saw on display a completed glider unit that had been rebuilt by students at the Institute. (A glider unit is a partially completed truck that lacks the engine, transmission, rear axles, rear-axle suspension, batteries, rear wheels and tires, clutch, and drive shaft. Glider kits are used to rebuild damaged trucks or convert them. They provide a like-new tractor that is much cheaper than a new model w uld be.) Following the showing in Chicago, the glider was returned to the school for use in the truck driver training program.

The twenty-six students in the vocational class rebuilt two wrecked heavy truck chassis during their training program. They completely restored a cab-over model; they overhauled the power train on another and matched it with a conventional cab International Transtar glider kit.

If household moving interests you, consider Triton College in River Grove, Illinois. Triton is a state-accredited community college that offers a certificated course entitled "Long Distance Moving and Storage (Contract Owner-Operator)." The aim of the course is to teach you to become a contract owner-operator. The year-long program offers courses in Business Organization, Bookkeeping, Human Relations, Claim Prevention, and Tractor/Trailer Operation and Maintenance. You can take the courses full or part-time.

You should keep three things in mind so that you will not be disappointed in the school you choose. First, no school can guarantee you a job when the course is completed. Second, no school can turn out a fully experienced driver. No matter how fine the school you attend, there are some things you can learn only by driving day after day. Unfortunately some students do not master even the very basic driving skills presented in the training programs.

Finally, there are other factors in addition to driving ability that determine if you will be hired. Your appearance, your personality, and your ability to get along with others influence prospective employers. B. W. Preston of the Texas State Technical Institute advises prospective trucking students to consider carefully their abilities and desires for trucking *before* committing themselves to a driver training program.

Let's suppose you have had some practical experience around trucks. You've attended a reputable driving school. You are ready to find a job. Where should you look? Start at the nearest trucking terminal.

Prospective employers have different ways of selecting safe, reliable drivers. Some use aptitude tests. Others hire on the basis of a personal interview.

You may have to begin your job as a helper to a local driver. Your job may be to assist in loading and unloading. Occasionally you will be given the opportunity to do some relief driving. It's important to have some experience in local trucking before attempting the long hauls. As you gain experience, you will be given the opportunity to drive larger, more complicated trucks for greater distances.

Drivers employed by common carriers frequently start on the "extra board." That's a list of drivers, assigned in rotation, who substitute for regular drivers or who make extra trips when they are needed. A new driver can bid for regular runs on the basis of seniority when vacancies occur.

You should accept a job as co-driver at the first opportunity. Don't be too proud to be an assistant. You'll find that driving an eighteen wheeler is worth every last ounce of effort it takes to persuade someone to give you a chance to drive. You should spend a minimum of one year working with an experienced professional driver before you think about striking out on your own. Many companies require as much as three years of driving experience before they will hire you. It is true that every company wants *experienced* drivers. (But some will settle for less.) Don't get impatient! In three years' time you can learn much from working with and observing an experienced professional behind the wheel. It's cheaper to learn on someone else's equipment, too!

It is possible that after making all of the preparations, you will decide you don't want the responsibilities of driving a big rig. Don't panic. All of your training and road experience will put you in good stead to obtain another job in the trucking industry. You haven't wasted your time. You are in a position to understand many phases of the industry. By now you have compiled a good record with your present employer who will be happy to give you a recommendation for another trucking job. He knows you know what trucking is all about.

Chances are, though, that after a few years on the road, you are madly in love with those powerful diesels and nothing short of a national disaster can keep you away from them. You're old enough and have had enough experience to qualify for a number of driving positions. If you like the security of working for

A proud driver teams this Mack R 600 conventional.

someone else and not having the worries and responsibilities of ownership of the business, keep on trucking as a company driver.

But if you've just "gotta" have your own rig, maybe you are ready for it now. Consider the responsibilities of the owner-operator. Be sure you have enough cash for the down payment and for working capital until your truck is paid for. According to William D. McLean of the Motor Vehicle Manufacturers Association, this is a super high risk venture. In the past three or four years, thousands of owner-operators have gone bankrupt. But others make a success of it. Know for whom you will work and what you will pull before you choose your equipment. Talk with others who work for the company you plan to work for to see what they think about their jobs. If all of the signals are "Go," then jump in. The plunge you are about to take is a giant one. Don't make a big splash and then sink!

WHAT IS AN OWNER-OPERATOR?

One of the most important decisions you will make if you become a trucker is whether to work for a company and drive its equipment or to become an owner-operator. An owner-operator is an independent businessman who owns his own truck. He is his own manager, engineer, accountant, lawyer, financier, buyer, salesman, mechanic, personnel director, and driver.

The American Trucking Associations, Inc. estimates there are 100,000 owner-operators on the highways today. About half of these are under long-term contracts to drive for companies. Ray Byler, whom you met earlier in this book, is an independent owner-operator leased to Mason and Dixon.

Becoming an owner-operator is the goal of many a driver, but only about one in four makes it. Why? What does it take to succeed? First of all it takes generous financial assets and a businessman's head, or tremendous borrowing capacity. Writing in *Overdrive* magazine (June, 1977), Ms. Donna Tracy of Apollo Truck Brokerage states that an independent trucker has an initial investment of about $75,000 in his tractor and trailer alone, to say nothing of the outlandish amounts of money he pays for taxes, licenses, and insurance. There is a high turnover rate in this field because too many do not have enough money or business sense to succeed.

Brant Clark, executive editor of the magazine, *Owner Operator*, suggests the following formula for determining how much cash is essential to become an independent driver. Take the amount needed for a down payment of the truck. Add to it the costs of licenses, insurance for one year, and permits. Now take that total and double it. If you were to buy a $12,000 used rig, you would need $9,300 to begin if you were to follow this sound formula.

If you buy a new tractor, of course the costs will be proportionately higher. If this sounds like too much money, remember you need money to buy the rig, to operate it, and to live. Undercaptialization is the greatest cause of business failure.

As an owner-operator, you must know how to take care of your equipment. You need to know how to prevent problems from developing. You have to be able to repair your own rig, so you should have a better-than-average mechanical ability.

You must understand federal and state laws, weight and

Even a used rig requires a lot of capital investment. Mike O'Brien (left), manager of International Harvester's Used Truck Center at Melrose Park, Illinois, discusses the merits of this Ford engine with a potential customer.

Preventative maintenance is the rule for success. Ray Byler spends much of his nondriving time checking out his rig.

length limits, fuel and highway user taxes, licensing, permits, state reciprocity agreements, and operating limitations. You have to know how to file reports, fill out tax forms, and keep your driver's log book accurately.

To be successful you need to understand basic bookkeeping. You have to handle money and budget for maintenance, operation, vehicle payments, and living expenses. You must be able to figure your cost per mile, and to keep records to insure that you are operating profitably. You have to understand costs and how to make a profit. You need to be able to read your contracts.

You have to know what kind of an operation or commodity

An owner-operator must understand federal and state laws, regulations, and limitations. Dave Irvin, independent owner, brushes up on a few points.

It takes time and know-how to keep your own truck running efficiently.

pays the best and where to find it. You must learn how to get the best hauls and which ones to avoid. It's important to weigh all of these factors to determine if you should haul for a fleet or as an independent driver.

Besides the head knowledge that is absolutely essential for success, you have to have operating skills that come only through long hours behind the wheel. You must be able to handle different types of equipment under varied circumstances. You need to be able to back, turn in congested areas, climb grades, pull out of holes, run on slick surfaces, make emergency stops, and handle panic situations.

As an independent driver, you must spend long periods of time away from home. When you return home, you will be kept busy working on your rig to keep it running properly.

If you are married, you need to have an understanding spouse. If you can persuade your marriage partner to join you as a co-driver, your marriage will take on a new dimension as together you see the country and meet new challenges. If your spouse rejects the idea of traveling with you on the road and isn't happy with the thought of holding second place in your heart—next to your truck—then you had better think three times before investing in that big tractor.

Why would anyone want to become an owner-operator if it is such a demanding profession? A big reason is pride. Pride in one's self and in the ability to handle thousands of dollars' worth of one's own equipment and someone else's goods.

As an independent trucker, you can choose your own equipment. What you drive is subject only to two considerations: what you plan to haul and how much money you have to spend on your equipment. If a White Road Boss 2 is the only thing to make you happy, then you can get a White Road Boss 2. No one can dictate to an independent what kind of rig he will team.

As an independent trucker, you can choose where and when you will work. If you can't take any more sleet, blizzards, or icy roads, no one will stop you if you decide to do your trucking south of the Mason-Dixon line. If you have gypsy blood in your veins, you can choose to haul those commodities that take you

The proudest driver of all is the independent owner-operator as he "bogie-bogies" down the highway.

back and forth across the United States with trips that are six weeks in duration. You can be one of those many drivers who average 100,000 miles per year. And all along the way you can enjoy the sights from high up in your Chevrolet Bison or whatever tractor you choose for your very own.

Not the least advantage in being an owner-operator is the fact that you will make more money than the hired driver.

If you are an experienced trucker with a heart for adventure, a head for figures, and a substantial bank account, go ahead and join the proudest of all teamsters, the independent owner-operators.

6

KNIGHTS OF THE ROAD

GOOD SAMARITAN TRUCKER

The newlyweds were enroute from Minnesota to Montana when they were plagued with a series of car troubles. Because the repairs were so costly, they found themselves out of cash with nearly two hundred miles to go and their gasoline gauge reading empty. Since they were from out of state, no one would cash their personal check.

Knowing the reputation truck drivers have for lending a helping hand, they broke for the eighteen wheeler that had been following them. They explained their problem to the driver and asked him if he would take a check for ten dollars so that they could buy gasoline. The trucker agreed. He promised to follow them to the next town and cash the check there for them.

A short time later the three met at a small restaurant. The trucker insisted that the young folks accompany him inside where he bought them supper. As they got ready to continue their journey, he handed them twenty dollars. He would not take their check. His kindness and his generosity will never be forgotten by that young couple who knew they could count on a trucker being a good Samaritan.

TRUCKER PUTS LIFE ON THE LINE

Truckers also have a reputation for helping even when to do so puts their own lives in danger. Harold Delaney, a motorist from Cormorack, New York, witnessed one brave trucker in action when a truck caught fire near Blue Ash, Ohio.

The trucker who came upon the scene thought the driver was still in the truck. He rushed up to the cab, smashed in a window, cut himself with the glass, and burned his hand when he grabbed the hot door handle. Small explosions were going on and nobody else dared to go near the truck. The concerned trucker sprayed the cab with his fire extinguisher and searched for the driver.

"When he found nobody in the truck, he just quietly walked away. His shirt was burned off his back and a wire was jammed through one of his fingers," said Delaney, who was awed by such a display of heroism.

The police who investigated the accident discovered the driver had escaped unharmed from the burning truck and had run to summon help. The would-be rescuer remained a nameless, unsung hero.

A DOUBLE RESCUE BY "THE DOUBLE EAGLE"

The date was December 13, 1973. Wayne Ramsey from Denison, Texas, known to his CB friends as "The Double Eagle," was teaming his eighteen wheeler home from California in the wee hours of the morning. As he neared the city limits of Abilene, he spotted a truck overturned and burning beside Interstate 20. Wayne braked his rig, jumped out, and dashed toward the flaming wreckage. "The driver's still inside!" yelled a horrified bystander. Without hesitation Wayne lunged through the broken windshield and found the driver, Kenny Langlinais, pinned by his steering wheel.

"Get my wife out! She's in the sleeper!" Langlinais screamed. Braving the flames and the heat, Wayne charged through the narrow opening leading into the sleeper behind the cab. The fire had already spread into the sleeper and had ignited Mrs. Langlinais' clothing. Wayne pulled the terrified lady from the holocaust and dashed back to the cab. He found the anguished driver holding his pocket knife in his hands.

"Cut my legs off, but get me out," he pleaded. The fire was spreading. Cartridges from a pistol inside the cab were exploding. So were the cans of hair spray that made up the truck's cargo. Nevertheless Wayne managed to keep his head, free the driver, and drag him to safety.

"There's little doubt that the quick action on the part of Wayne Ramsey saved the lives of Mr. and Mrs. Langlinais," said Abilene policeman Wylie B. Walker, who investigated the accident.

In the fall of 1975, "The Double Eagle" received a check for $1,000 and the Carnegie Medal in recognition of his outstanding heroism as he risked his own life in order to save two others from death.

TRUCKER ANSWERS DESPERATE PLEA FOR HELP

Wallace Chapman was in a hurry to get his load of soft drink bottles from the Chattanooga Glass Company to its Louisiana destination. He had slept an hour longer than he had planned, so he had to hustle. Then he heard a weak voice on his CB, the voice of a stranger in distress.

"Help me . . . Please help me . . . I'm in trouble." The voice was faint and sounded very troubled.

Though he was only 250 miles out of Chattanooga, Wallace felt somebody needed his help worse than the bottling company needed those bottles. He found a place to turn around and began searching for the stranger. "This is one load of freight that will have to wait," he said to himself.

Meanwhile, about seventeen miles from Tuscaloosa, Alabama, Eddie Burger had pulled his rig over to the side of the road. He had been hit earlier with waves of nausea. Now he was hemorrhaging heavily from a bleeding ulcer. He was too weak to move from his cab. He tried repeatedly to summon help on the emergency channel of his CB radio. He watched helplessly as many drivers passed him by unaware of his desperate situation. He grew weaker as the bleeding continued.

"The next thing I remember was the smiling face of Wallace Chapman," he recalls.

Wallace not only summoned an ambulance after checking out Eddie's condition, but he also washed him down with cold water, and kept him talking. Later he drove Eddie's rig to a nearby truck stop and locked it up for him.

Eddie Burger spent three days in intensive care and then underwent surgery. His doctors acknowledged that help had come just in time.

When Wallace returned to Chattanooga he learned what had happened to the man he had rescued on Interstate 59. "I didn't know he was at Memorial Hospital until his boss called me and thanked me for taking care of his driver," said Wallace. In no time he was at the hospital visiting the man whose life he had saved by his unselfishness, his quick thinking, and his knowledge of first aid.

KIDNAP SUSPECT CAPTURED WITH TRUCKERS' HELP

Two southern truck drivers, using their CB radios, helped police in southern Georgia capture a Florida prison escapee who had kidnapped a woman in late January of 1976. The escapee broke into a High Springs residence, kidnapped the woman, and drove away in her car.

A trucker, known as "Double E," spotted the vehicle near the Florida-Georgia line shortly after a description of the stolen car went out over the CB radio. He enlisted the help of a fellow trucker, the "Carolina Country Boy," and together they boxed the car in between them. Then they contacted the Georgia State Patrol.

In an effort to shake off the truckers, the escapee pulled off Interstate 75 onto a rest stop. The truckers followed suit and blocked the entrance and the exit. The prisoner surrendered quietly when police officers arrived shortly thereafter. The kidnap victim was found tied in the back seat. She had been severely beaten, but was in fair condition.

TRUCKERS TRAP YOUTHFUL IOWA ROBBERS

It seemed a very normal run for Paul Puggle and Harley Steinhoek as they teamed their eighteen wheelers south on Interstate 35 headed toward Webster City. They were running together with their "ears" on when their conversation was interrupted by a patrol officer breaking to give the description of a getaway car. Instinctively each driver glanced into his mirrors.

"Sounds like we've got us a little excitement in town tonight, huh?"

"I guess so. Wonder how much loot they got away with."

The trucks were just passing the Dows Interchange. "Say . . . will you look at that baby that just drove on! Doesn't that four wheeler fit the description we just heard?"

"I'd say it's a pretty good match. Do you want to report it?"

"Ten-four."

"Breaker, one-nine. I think we've got your baby at our back door."

"Thanks, Good Buddy. What's your twenty?"

"We've just passed the Dows Interchange."

"Can you keep him in sight till we catch up with you?"

"Ten-four. We sure will try. There happens to be two of us running together. We'll see what we can do."

Keeping their eyes on the car behind them, the drivers planned their strategy. In a moment Harley's left-turning signal came on and he deftly eased his big rig out from behind his buddy and pulled up beside him. The getaway car also pulled into the passing lane. Then, much to the driver's frustration, the trucker slowed down. The big rigs continued down the interstate side by side, despite the frantic efforts of the four wheeler to get Harley to pull over and let him by.

As soon as the truckers saw the patrol car behind them, they slowed their trucks to a stop right there on the interstate. Very shortly the young thieves were taken into custody. Officer Hintch thanked the truckers for their help in apprehending the suspects. Then Paul and Harley continued on their way, glad to have had some excitement on what had been a routine run.

7

THE CB RADIO AND
TRUCKERS' JARGON

Citizens Band radio is a radio-telephone system. It uses radio waves to carry your voice from one place to another. It is similar to the radio units that have been used by taxi drivers and patrol cars for many years. CB is almost like a telephone, a wireless party line. It has done much to alleviate the lonesomeness of the long-distance driver. It gives him someone to talk with as he streaks along into the night.

Besides relieving the monotony of a long trip, CB is also used extensively to warn of traffic tie-ups, wrecks, emergency vehicles heading your way, and other people in trouble. It is a quick source of information when you are lost, or in need of some kind of assistance on the highway.

In 1973 many truckers installed CB units in their rigs because of the fuel shortage. They had to know where they could find fuel to keep rolling. The reduced speed limit to 55 mph created

Citizens Band radio is widely used for fun as well as business.

more problems. The CB rigs kept drivers informed of radar traps and they were able to make their deadlines for deliveries.

The plight of the truckers was a serious one. They knew they must do something drastic to get the public eye and enforce changes if they were to stay in business. They were incensed not only by the fuel scarcity, but by its increasing cost. The sudden imposition of the new speed limit was the last straw. On January 31, 1974, some drivers pulled their eighteen wheelers into strategic locations. They blocked interchanges, accesses, and interstates across the country. Then they switched off their engines and walked away. This nationwide show of consternation was coordinated through CB radio. The whole country began to ask questions. What is CB? they wanted to know, when they realized it was the key to this unified action.

Soon the public began buying sets. By 1977 there were more than 15 million owners of CB radios in the United States.

CB users began to sense a feeling of belonging, as though they were members of a clique. They were friends who were ready to help one another. They called each other "Good Buddy," though they had never met. They used their sets to share conversation. CB was welcomed as a means of bridging the communications gap between individuals. It was like saying to the person on the other end, "I am out here listening to you because I want to hear what you have to say to me." That kind of sharing was fun to the trucker, so he kept on talking even after the initial crisis that triggered his interest in the CB radio had passed.

What is CB talk? It's more than a language. It's a whole new way of expressing one's thoughts. The editors of *Elementary Electronics* describe it as an unlikely mixture of highway, police, and military slang. To "modulate" like an old "biscuit burner" means to talk like an old pro on your CB unit. The proper accent, the correct tone of voice, and the speed of delivery combine to make you sound like an honest-to-goodness eighteen wheeler, or a well-seasoned CBer. That is, if you also use the correct terms.

The over-the-road truckers were the first to use CB radio extensively. They had no time for lengthy refined conversation as they "jammed the gears" en route to a distant terminal. Their talk was terse and blunt. It was humorous, too. CBers who listened to the truckers converse adopted and sometimes adapted their speech. Today it's difficult to distinguish between CB language and truckers' jargon. Some words vary in their meaning as one travels from coast to coast. The mini-glossary that follows is a combination of phrases from the truckers and the CB users throughout our country.

Truck drivers who are CBers as well are quick to respond to emergency calls on their sets. They are ready to render assistance or communicate emergency situations to the police and/or rescue squads. Some of them belong to an agency called HART—Highway Aid by Radio Truck. HART members are truck drivers who have been taught emergency aid techniques. Since they are experienced drivers, they possess auto repair ability as well.

Other drivers are members of REACT—Radio Emergency Associated Citizens Team. During their off hours they help monitor Channel 9, the emergency channel. They relay calls to the local police, hospitals, and others as emergency situations demand.

You can read about emergencies alleviated through CB users in nearly any CB magazine or trucking journal you pick up. In the section of this book entitled "Knights of the Road" there are a number of incidents related in which truckers engineered the rescue operations. Many times the drivers learned of the emergency through their "squawk box" and used it to handle the situation quickly and effectively.

The following list of words and phrases with their definitions will help you understand what is being said when you are listening to a CB transmission. (You're "sandbagging" when you do that.) If you want a more comprehensive list, write to the American Trucking Associations, Inc., Education Section, 1616 P Street, Washington, D.C. 20036, and ask for the *Truck Drivers Dictionary and Glossary*. It is free.

A GLOSSARY OF CB AND TRUCKERS' JARGON

Advertising—A marked police car with its lights on.
Anchor it—To apply brakes for an emergency stop.
Aviator—A speeding driver.
Back door—The last vehicle in a line moving in a group.
Back down—To reduce speed.
Back out—To sign off CB transmission.
Bareback—A tractor without a semi-trailer.
Barefoot—An unmodified CB rig.
Bear—Any police officer.
Beat the bushes—The first vehicle in a convoy watching for speed traps and traffic tie-ups.
Big ten-four—I agree 100 percent.
Bleedover—Signals from the next channel being heard on your channel.
Bob tail—A tractor cab without a trailer; bareback.
Bodacious—A really great signal.
Body—Semi-trailer.
Bogie-bogie—To drive a truck.

Box—The semi-trailer, or body, of a truck.

Bubble machine—A patrol car with light and siren mounted on its roof.

Cab—The portion of the truck where the driver sits.

Cab-over—A vehicle with a major part of its engine located under the cab.

Cackle crate—A truck that hauls live poultry.

Catch you on the flip-flop—I'll see you on the return trip.

Clean—There's no police car in the area.

Clear—I'm finishing my transmitting.

COE—A cab-over-engine tractor.

Coffee break—An informal gathering of CBers.

Coffin box—A sleeper compartment independent of the truck cab.

Comic books—Truck driver's log sheets.

Common carrier—A trucking company that hauls goods for anyone who has the money to pay for the service.

Concrete slab—The superhighway.

Contract carrier—A trucking company that contracts to haul goods exclusively for a specific company or a limited number of companies.

Cotton picker—A CBer you don't like.

County mounty—A sheriff's deputy.

Cut out—To leave the channel.

Conventional—A tractor with the engine located in front of the driver's compartment.

Dayton wheels—Spoke wheels on a tractor.

Deadheading—Running empty.

Dock it—To park the truck at the dock.

Dolly—The supporting gear that holds up the front end of a semi when it is parked without the tractor.

Double nickles—The 55 mph limit.

Down time—The time a truck spends off the road in the terminal or repair shop.

Double-clutcher—A driver who shifts gears without clashing them by pumping the clutch twice.

Drop the body—To unhook and drive a tractor away from a parked semi.

Drop the hammer—To accelerate to top speed.

Ears—Antennas, or other pieces of communications equipment.

Ears on—Listening to your CB set.

Eighteen wheeler—Any tractor trailer combination with eighteen wheels.

Eights and other good numbers—I'm ending my transmission.

Feed the bears—To get a speeding ticket.

Fifth wheel—A circular device used to connect a tractor to a semi.

Foot warmer—An illegal linear amplifier.

Four wheeler—A passenger vehicle.

Front door—The lead truck in a convoy of trucks.

Gearjammer—One who constantly clashes the gears; any truck driver.

Getting out—Being heard by others on the CB.

Gone—To leave a channel.

Good Buddy—What you call a friend over the air.

Green stamps—Money paid for fines.

Gypsy—An independent trucker who drives his own truck and secures freight wherever he can.

Hammer down—To be running at top speed.

Handle—The nickname you use on CB.

Hauling post holes—Driving an empty truck or trailer.

Holler—To call another station by CB radio.

Hood lifter—A garage mechanic.

Home 20—The location of a mobile unit's base station.

In the grass—Located on the median strip.

ICC—The Interstate Commerce Commission, the federal rule-making body which regulates the trucking industry.

Jackknife—An accident which places the trailer at a sharp angle to the tractor, caused by sudden swerves or a fast stop on a wet or icy road.

Jump the pin—To miss the fifth wheel pin on the trailer when coupling the tractor to the trailer.

Jamboree—A gathering of CBers, dealers, or manufacturers.

Kidney buster—A hard-riding truck.

K-Whopper—A Kenworth tractor.

Landline—The telephone.

Lay over—To take a rest of eight of more hours before continuing a trip.

Linehaul driver—A trucker who has a regularly scheduled route; also called a line driver.

Local yokel—A small town or city police officer.

Mail—Conversation on a CB channel.

Mercy—Wow!

Milepost—Markers along major highways.

Mobile—A CB station located in a vehicle.

Modulate—To speak to another CBer.

Negative—No.

Negative contact—Nobody answered my call.

Negative copy—I can't understand your transmission.

Negatory—No.

On the side—Not in motion; also, listening to someone else's conversation and joining in once in a while.

Over—It's your turn to transmit.

Over-the-road driver—A driver hauling goods long distances.

Over your shoulder—Directly behind you.

Payload—The freight that a truck hauls.

Peanut butter in your ears—Said of a CBer who can't copy a transmission.

"Pete"—A Peterbilt tractor.

Picture taker—A radar speed trap.

Piggyback—A transportation system where trailers are carried by rail.

Possum belly—A livestock trailer with a drop frame for hauling small animals (like pigs or chickens) underneath heavy cattle.

Private carrier—A firm which trucks its own raw materials or finished products, though trucking is not the company's main business activity.

Put the good numbers on you—Best regards. Said at the end of a CB transmission.

Radio check—A test with another station to see if equipment is working properly.

Rake the leaves—To be on the lookout for police, speed traps, or traffic tie-ups as the first truck in a convoy.

Ratchet jaw—A CBer who can't seem to stop talking; also called a "bucket mouth."

REACT—Radio Emergency Associated Citizens Team.

Reefer—A refrigerated truck or trailer designed for hauling perishables.

Ride shotgun—To ride on the right side of the cab.

Rig—A truck, a tractor semi-trailer combination; a CB unit.

Rocking chair—Any vehicle in the middle of a convoy.

Roger—Okay.

Seatcovers—Passengers in a car, especially girls.

Semi—A semi-trailer; can also mean a tractor and its trailer.

Set it down—To stop quickly.

Seventy-threes—Best regards.

Shake the leaves—To watch for police as you bring up the rear in a convoy.

Shake the lights—To blink headlights to warn other drivers.

Shout—To call another CB operator on the air.

Skins—Tires.

Skip—Station located at a great distance whose signals are heard by means of atmospheric conditions.

Sleeper—A truck cab with a sleeping compartment.

Smoke him—To pass another vehicle.

Smokey the Bear—Any police officer.

Spash over (splatter)—Signals leaking over from adjacent channels; bleedover.

Spot—To park a rig.

Spotter—A terminal yard driver who parks vehicles brought in by regular drivers.

Strip her—To unload a trailer.

Superslab—A superhighway.

Swindle sheet—A log book.

Taking pictures—Using radar.

Tandem—A semi-trailer or tractor with two rear axles.

Team—To drive a big rig.

Teamster—A unionized truck driver.

Ten-four—Okay. I agree.

Ten wheeler—A tandem-axle trailer.

Tijuana taxi—A marked police car.

Tooling down the highway—Driving at normal speed.

Twin-screw—A truck or tractor with two rear axles, both driven by the engine.

Wall-to-wall—A super powerful CB signal.

Wall-to-wall bears—Strict enforcement of speed limits; or a high concentration of police and radar.

Waybill—The list of goods and shipping instructions given to the common carrier.

We gone—We've stopped transmitting; we're just listening now.

Wind deflector—A device mounted on the roof of the tractor to reduce aerodynamic drag; also called an airshield or dynafoil.

Woodchuck—Driver with low job seniority.

Wrapper—The color of a vehicle, especially a patrol car.

Yardbird—A driver who connects and disconnects tractor semi-trailer combinations and moves vehicles around the terminal yard.

Yard mule—A small tractor used to move semi-trailers around the terminal yard.

8

INCENTIVES FOR GOOD DRIVING

There must be something very rewarding about driving a truck. Otherwise how can we account for the 850,000 drivers crisscrossing our highways each day? What keeps them at their wheels?

For some it is merely a means of earning a living. But for the majority, it is an exciting way of life. As one long-distance driver put it, "We are fiercely proud of our trucks and our jobs." It's that kind of tenacious pride that keeps the wheels rolling. Many a driver finds a keen personal satisfaction in his own safety record, and there is an increasing number of companies that recognize their drivers when they have completed great numbers of accident-free miles.

In the spring of 1976, Neal Foster, a fifty-four-year-old grandfather from Davenport, Iowa, completed three million miles of safe driving. Foster has been driving for Carstensen Freight

Lines for thirty-five years. He pilots an International COF 4070B Transtar II tractor. His tour of duty begins each afternoon at Rock Island, Illinois. He travels between Chicago and Cedar Rapids, Iowa, nightly, with stops at Clinton, Iowa, the home office, and Sterling, Illinois.

"Driving today is a lot easier than it was when I started many years ago," observes Foster. "Both roads and equipment are a lot better."

Foster's first truck was a 1937 D-35 International. As an owner-operator driving strictly for Carstensen, he began his safe driving in a succession of International trucks. Since switching from an owner-operator to a Carstensen-employed driver, Foster has driven cab-over, heavy-duty models.

His driving record did not just happen. Foster is concerned with safety. "I always try to drive ahead of myself. I don't let myself become distracted. Good driving demands concentration.

"I keep looking behind me as well as ahead. I try to know what's happening on all sides of the truck and trailer at all times. If I have to make an emergency stop, I need to know what the consequences of that stop will be.

Neal Foster (left) discusses his upcoming run to Chicago with Carstensen operations manager, Ron Mallicoat.

"Accidents don't just happen. I've pulled enough people out of wrecks to know what the results of a single act of carelessness can be."

Foster's outstanding driving record earned him the title "Iowa Driver of the Month" in 1968, and "Illinois Driver of the Month" in 1975.

Parkhill Truck Company, a subsidiary of Tri-State Motor Transit Company, began its Safety Award Program in January, 1973. It bases its awards on nonchargeable accident miles that each driver accrues—no accidents that were his fault. Dan R. Shugart, a tractor trailer over-the-road driver since 1953, was the first driver with his company to drive 400,000 miles without a chargeable accident (one that the driver might have prevented) since the program began. Shugart was presented a Bulova Acutron wristwatch in recognition of his safety record. Shugart, who lives in Medford, Oregon, has driven approximately two million miles in the past twenty-five years.

In addition to being honored by their companies for their personal achievement, many drivers earn recognition as "Driver of the Year" for their companies or in their home states. Albert L. Mead, a driver for Consolidated Freightways, Inc., of Tonawanda, New York, was honored for his eight years of safe driving for Consolidated and given special recognition for his heroism in trying to save four college students trapped in their burning camper.

Mead was headed toward home from Providence, Rhode Island, about midnight on June 7, 1974, when his truck was passed by a camper. A few miles later he saw the camper swerve and overturn. By the time he could stop his semi and get to the wrecked camper, it burst into flames. It was lying on the door side, cutting off any chance for the occupants to escape. Mead attempted to break the windshield with a crowbar to free the screaming students. About that time the camper exploded, throwing him to the pavement. Picking himself up, he attacked the windshield a second time, but was driven back by the intense heat. By the time the Turnpike emergency vehicle arrived, it was too late to do anything for the four young people. Mead was treated for burns and cuts at the scene and later resumed his trip to Buffalo.

In recognition of this attempt to rescue the unfortunate victims, Mead was named "New York State Driver of the Year."

TRUCK DRIVER OF THE YEAR

One of the greatest honors a truck driver can receive is being named "Truck Driver of the Year" by the American Trucking Associations, Inc. Olen "Oley" Lee Welk of Big Dandy, Texas, earned that title in 1977. He was the thirtieth winner of the contest that began in 1947 as part of a national courtesy and safety campaign. At that time state motor carrier associations were encouraged to select drivers of the month and name drivers

Olen Lee Welk, American Trucking Associations' "Truck Driver of the Year" for 1977

of the year. Many still follow that custom.

Oley Welk had won the driver of the year award in Texas and in Missouri prior to his national honor. ATA chose him because of his outstanding safety record as well as for his act of heroism. Oley, at the time of the honor, had logged more than 3.5 million miles without a preventable accident. To date he has been trucking for forty-two years, twenty-six of them for C & H Transportation Company, Inc., of Dallas.

In 1958 he was named "Knight of the Road" by the Hobbs Trailer Company. On one of his trips he came upon an over-turned car in which the driver had died, leaving thousands of dollars in his wallet. Oley fended off would-be thieves and turned the driver's wallet and cash over to the Texas Highway Patrol.

Besides the personal satisfaction he feels in knowing he is a good driver, Welk received a trophy and a diamond pin from the Federal Highway Administrator in recognition of his national driver status.

Oley considers trucking a great life, a continuous adventure which he loves. "I wouldn't retire if I had $40 million," he says.

QUEEN OF THE ROAD

Lady drivers of big rigs can vie for the title of "Queen of the Road." To be eligible for this title, which is sponsored by *Open Road* magazine and conferred each year, they must be qualified drivers with a minimum of two years of truck driving experience. They must be fully licensed by their home states to drive a heavy-duty tractor and trailer.

Judging is on the basis of ability, experience, intelligence, and beauty. Drivers are nominated through letters which tell why the nominee should be named queen and which enclose her picture. A select board of judges considers the nominees and makes the decision.

The winner of the contest is given many prizes and appears throughout the year at major trucking shows. She is honored at a coronation dinner. Later she is the honored guest at the Superstar

Athletic Competition where she is given a special Superstar Trophy.

The first "Queen of the Road" was Linda Jean Jernigan, a native Floridian and a happy mother of two. The "Florida Mermaid," as she calls herself on CB, is an accomplished driver in a family of truckers. Since 1975 when she reigned as the first queen, she has been performing a dual role. Besides being half of a husband/wife owner-operator team, she is car care counselor for Fram/Autolite Corporation. The counselor program is geared specifically toward young motorists. Linda spends much of her time talking to driver education classes in public schools. She usually gets the attention of the class by pulling into the school parking lot in a gigantic rig. Her educational message to youth stresses safety and self-sufficiency on the highway.

Geri Atherton of Sacramento, California, was the 1976 "Queen of the Road." Geri is not only a trucker, but she also is music director of Radio Station K-POP outside Sacramento and has her own disc jockey program.

Cassandra "Sandi" Ramsburg Purdum, a twenty-seven-year-old dump truck driver, from Walkersville, Maryland, was named

Sandi Purdum, "Queen of the Road" for 1977

"Queen of the Road" for 1977. Ms. Purdum drives for Mitchell Transport, Inc., out of its Woodsboro, Maryland, terminal. She holds a Maryland Class A license, and has had eight years of trucking experience. Currently she is hauling aggregate, a burnt shale product which is used in making cement blocks. Bob Myers, regional manager for Mitchell Transport, says about Sandi, "She does the same job as the men do, and does it well. She's a very good driver and a person of fine character."

Sandi Purdum is a petite five-foot-two blonde and weighs 118 pounds. She has dazzling blue-green eyes.

Truck driving is an almost all-consuming passion for Sandi, but she is also an aspiring writer and a commissioned artist, according to Eileen Bagwell, Midwest editor of *Traffic World*, who nominated Sandi for "Queen of the Road." Sandi's poetry is chiefly about truck driving and about nature and love. She does her painting when business is slow.

In an interview with *Open Road*, Sandi said of herself, "I believe in women driving trucks. I'm glad that someone has done something for women drivers. It's a fact that I had to claw tooth and nail to get someone to hire me as a truck driver. But I am not a women's libber."

NOT ONLY DRIVERS ARE HONORED

If it weren't for the proper maintenance, trucks could not keep rolling. Recognizing this truth, the National Automobile Transportation Association chooses a "Maintenance Man of the Year." Selected for that honor in 1976 was Alfred Spong, Director of Maintenance for Motorcar Transport Company, in Pontiac, Michigan. Spong has been in the transportation industry for twenty-eight years and has headed up Motorcar's maintenance for the past twenty-five years.

THE ROADEO

You know what a rodeo is, with bucking broncos, calf roping, and shouts of "Ride 'em, Cowboy!" In the early days of the West, cattle and horses roamed the open range. Once a year all of the stock had to be rounded up and driven to a central place where the owners claimed what belonged to them. When all the stock had been claimed, the cowboys held a celebration, a rodeo. The public came to watch them perform tests of great skill as part of the celebration.

Rodeos are still held, to the delight of great audiences. However, a new form of entertainment is the "Roadeo." The performers in this event are not cowboys, but truck drivers. They are just as skillful in handling their giant tractor trailers as the cowboys are in twirling their lariats.

The national roadeos are sponsored by the American Trucking Associations, Inc., and are held annually to determine the top operators of commercial vehicles.

Many fleet owners hold roadeos to give their professional drivers a chance to test their job skills. The winners earn the privilege of competing in the statewide contests. State finalists go on to national drive-offs where winners are chosen in seven classes ranging from conventional two-axle units to huge and tricky double-bottom rigs.

To compete in a national roadeo, a driver has to be a full-time professional employed for at least a year by a licensed motor freight carrier. He must have an accident-free record for the past year and be in good all-round health.

The national competition is an intense one. At stake is peer recognition and a certain prestige which means more to many drivers than the trophies, plaques, and cash awards.

Let's see just how the competition is run. Before the actual driving begins, the participants must take three tests. The first is a personal interview. It evaluates the driver's appearance, personality, and attitudes. The second is a series of four written exams dealing with safe-driving practices, the trucking industry, first aid, and fire fighting. The third test grades the driver on his ability to check out his vehicle as he would do in a pre-trip inspection. About eighty items have to be checked. The driver is scored on his ability to spot "planted" defects as well as on his overall inspection efficiency.

Parallel Parking

The standard roadeo problems

Alley Dock

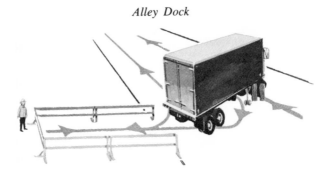

Offset Alley

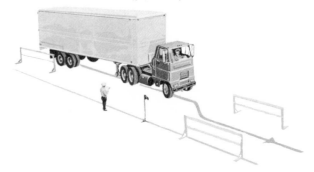

The Serpentine

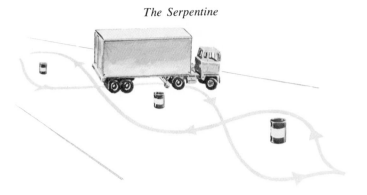

The Straight Line

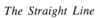

The Stop Line

The trucks used in the roadeo competition are new models that are provided by local dealers. The drivers choose one of seven classes in which to compete: straight truck; three, four, or five-axle semi-trailer; flatbed trailer; tank trailer; or twin-trailer.

Now to the skills tests. Drivers are judged on their ability to perform six operations quickly and precisely. These are all the kinds of problems they might meet any day when they are delivering a load of goods to a customer.

The first test is *Parallel Parking*. The driver must back into a parking place parallel to a simulated curb, and within six inches of it.

The second is *Alley Docking*. It tests the ability to back a vehicle into a narrow space and stop with the rear of the vehicle within six inches of the back of the dock.

The *Offset Alley* test requires the driver to move his vehicle through one set of barricades, turn to the right or left, and proceed through a second set. He must not stop or touch the barricades.

In the *Serpentine* test the driver must drive a figure-eight pattern around a line of obstacles set in the middle of a marked street.

The ability to judge accurately the position of the right wheels and hold the vehicle in a *Straight Line* is the fifth test. This is one of the most difficult. It consists of a double row of small sponge balls set on rubber caster cups only slightly larger than golfers' tees. There are two inches of clearance on either side. The slightest touch will send the balls bouncing away. The driver must drive his right wheels between the rows. Points are lost for each ball touched.

The *Stop Line* is the final test. It judges the ability to stop within six inches of a line, such as a crosswalk.

Each of these tests requires skill and precision. Drivers must not strike a barricade or run over a boundary. They can't dislodge a ball or make an unauthorized stop. They must complete all of the tests within a certain time limit, which is usually eight to ten minutes.

Bill Kilpatrick, writing in *Popular Mechanics*, likened partici-

The driver must maneuver his big rig within six inches of the curb.

pation in the national roadeo to playing in baseball's World Series. Certainly it is the high point in a professional truck driver's life.

Before he drives his course, each contestant is introduced to the audience individually. Details of his personal life are given as well as his safety record and his past roadeo record. Chances are

The participating drivers are introduced to the audience individually, and a brief biographical sketch is given.

Drivers lose five points for touching, running over, or contacting a marker. Here a driver is congratulated for skillful completion of the test in 1975, in Indianapolis.

The driver of this tanker will be penalized for each dislodged ball.

Contestants receive points for each defect discovered and for their efficiency in inspecting their vehicles.

A 1975 contestant leans out to check his backing progress.

Dean Benham, a driver for Crouch Freight Systems, Elmwood, Kansas, negotiates a parking problem during the finals of the Three-Axle Semi-Trailer Class at the 1976 Roadeo in Fort Worth, Texas.

Benham is congratulated after winning the championship in a cab-over International Cargostar medium-duty model.

Judges check the progress of an International CO-4070 Transtar II competing in Twin Trailer Class at Fort Worth.

The winner of the "doubles" championship was Roger James Hatch, a driver for Advance United Expressway, Minneapolis, Minnesota. Frank Miller (right), manager for International Trucks' Fort Worth Sales and Service Center, congratulates him on his winning performance.

his entire family will be in attendance as guests of the driver's sponsor, dressed in identical uniforms bearing their names and the names of the companies for which the men work. It's truly a "moment in the sun" for Dad. If he wins the $1,000 first prize which is offered in each division, the victory is even sweeter.

The next time you see a driver sporting a distinctive belt buckle proclaiming him to be a roadeo champion, remember he represents the "cream of the crop" in professional drivers. He earned his title against stiff competition.

If you want to know when there will be a roadeo in your area, ask the truck dealer in your vicinity. If he doesn't know, he can find out for you.

OTHER INCENTIVES

Top-notch drivers are sometimes chosen for unusual jobs like hauling large machinery, a rocket part, a scientific instrument, or a statue. The photograph shows "Washington Crossing the Delaware." It is a three-dimensional, life-sized, 28-ton limestone interpretation of the famous Emmanuel Leutze painting on its way from Bedford, Indiana, to Washington Crossing, Pennsylvania. The statue was dedicated on July 5, 1976, at the very spot where Washington and his 2,599 soldiers crossed the ice-choked Delaware River on Christmas night, 1776.

The statue made its 850-mile journey on a 42-foot drop frame trailer. It was transported by a special red, white, and blue International Transtar heavy-duty truck by Moon Freight Lines of Blomington, Indiana. Ted Benckart, son of Moon's president, was the principal driver.

"The International Transtar II cab provided the drivers a lot more comfort than Washington and his men enjoyed," noted Robert McArdle, president of McArdle International, the Bloomington dealership which delivered the truck. "At least they could sit during the trip. According to the painting, George had to stand during the crossing," he joked.

The rig that pulled this unusual cargo was powered by a 290 hp V8 diesel engine. It had a thirteen-speed transmission, power

Washington crosses the Delaware by International Transtar II truck.

Mack power moves the Reuben Wells to its new home in Indianapolis.

steering, tandem drive rear axle, 84-inch BBC sleeper, and 164-inch wheelbase.

It took a mighty Mack to move the 550-ton locomotive, the Reuben Wells, to its new home in the Children's Museum in Indianapolis. The Reuben Wells was the largest and most powerful locomotive in the world when it was built in 1968. Seen in the photograph is a Mack R 600 tractor, owned and operated by the Underwood Transfer Company, Inc., Indianapolis.

Late in 1976 a team of two drivers piloted a 130-foot, 98-ton, 36-wheel tractor trailer 2,700 miles from Seattle to Hollywood, Alabama. The cargo was a girder to be used for an overhead

It took 36 wheels and a driver in both the front and the rear to carry this cargo.

crane at a nuclear reactor site. The rig was so long that it needed one driver over the front axle and another over the rear one. The ten-foot-wide rig could only travel during the daylight hours. The photograph shows what the 36-wheeled monster looked like.

9

WOMEN IN TRUCKING

The drivers who were honored as "Queens of the Road" were chosen because of their outstanding driving abilities as well as their personal qualities. There are many lady drivers who have proved their competency behind the wheel of a big rig during the past few years while driving alone or with their husbands.

When the Interstate Commerce Commission granted equal rights to women on the truckways, the phenomenon of husband/wife teams was made possible. Today numerous companies, especially in the long-haul moving business, encourage these teams to maintain their own tractor and to contract with them.

Bekins Van Lines Company, a subsidiary of the Bekins Company of Los Angeles, was one of the pioneers in encouraging these partnerships by guaranteeing a stated gross income to both the driver and his partner. The teams were so successful from the beginning that the company continues to encourage husbands and wives to drive together for them.

Lee Waters, president of the company, observes that it is usu-

Ladies like Sandi Purdum prove that women can become successful truck drivers.

ally the wife who sweats it out when the family moves, since the husband has had to go on ahead to the new home.

"There she is alone," he says, "when a couple of burly fellows show up at her door to move her furniture. If a mover comes with his uniformed wife she can make a tough day a little easier by telling her that moving to New York will be a great experience or that North Carolina really is a beautiful place to live."

Mary and Bill Britton of Tucson, Arizona, were one of the first couples to hit the road together for Bekins. "When word came down on the ICC decision, I immediately packed my bags, shut off the utilities, and took off," recalls Mary.

Mary is not a free-riding passenger clinging to her husband. She, like most wives who truck with their spouses, carries her share of responsibilities for driving, loading and unloading, and keeping up with the endless round of paperwork that federal and state agencies require.

Mary and Bill Britton

Muriel and Walt Bossert

The recession in 1975 put Muriel and Walt Bossert of San Diego, California, into business as contract drivers. When it looked like the recession would be prolonged, the couple began looking at business investments that would provide them with a good salary and long-term security. Although they knew nothing about trucks, they liked the economics of being a contract driver.

"Bekins helped us purchase a truck, paid for our licenses and related fees, and provided us the necessary training we needed," says Muriel. "Of course it took us a number of years to pay off our tractor loan and during that period there were lots of business expenses. Now that we own our tractor, our net income has increased considerably."

Some couples see escape from the formalities of social life as one of the greatest appeals of "movin' and truckin.' " Dick and Lisa Gazda of Minneapolis spent four years on the road together. Part of that time was shared in a $70,000 movable mansion.

"Our truck was our home," Lisa explained. "We lived in it. That's why we specified every option possible when we ordered it." Those options included a lavish interior equipped with AM/FM radio, stereo system, hand-stitched upholstery with complete padding, color TV, walnut cabinets, and reading lamps.

Dick estimates that he and Lisa covered 70,000 to 80,000 miles a year. He did the driving while Lisa managed the paperwork and helped him keep the log book. Being outside, traveling and meeting people during the highly personal process of moving, and being free of binding social commitments for a long period of time attracted the Gazdas to the unique life style. In 1977 the Gazdas decided to sell their luxury rig to another Bekins husband/wife team so that Dick could join his brothers in business with a Bekins' moving agency.

Julie Hall, the "Midnight Angel," is 4 feet 11 inches tall and tips the scales at 100 pounds. Yet this energetic little blonde manhandles loads reaching as much as 80,000 pounds. She and

Lisa and Dick Gazda

her husband are coast-to-coast drivers for the Melvin Strickland Company.

In addition to being a wife and mother of two small children, Julie is active in commercial art. Her artwork centers around designing jackets and patches for CB and trucking clubs. "I do this because I love to draw and design. It also helps break the tension of driving," she says.

When Julie is not driving, she operates a diesel control station from her home in Mount Airy, North Carolina. She uses a powerful two-way radio to do this. Her work consists of handling emergency calls and giving information to local traffic. Julie got her CB handle from a trucker she helped through her diesel control station.

TRUCKS, TRUCKING AND YOU   129

She decided to become a trucker when she was eighteen years old. A couple of experienced drivers became her advisors and helped her on her way.

"Trucks were big and becoming a driver presented a challenge I couldn't resist," she told an interviewer for Open Road. "Now that I'm where I am, I wouldn't change a thing."

The petite driver says her size is no handicap, but it does cause some inconveniences. A bump usually slams her head into the roof of the cab, since she has to raise the air seat so high to see out over the front end of the tractor.

Julie has this advice for girls who would like to become truck drivers. "As a trucker you will be a woman in a man's world. There are some things related to your truck that you simply cannot handle yourself. There are times when you have to have a man's advice and assistance. Don't be too proud to ask for either. Above all, take pride in your personal appearance. Be a lady. Dress like one, talk like one, and act like one. Then you will be treated as one. And if you need help, the men will be glad to come to your assistance."

Muriel and Kenneth Hayes are a unique husband/wife team. They are owner-operators driving for St. Lawrence Freightways, Inc. with headquarters in Watertown, New York. Unlike most teams who take turns driving the same rig, each drives his or her own truck. Muriel differs from many lady truckers in that she did not have to beg for a job driving. Instead, the terminal manager at St. Lawrence asked her to drive for his company.

"We didn't hire her because she was a woman, but because she is a competent driver," explained Charles A. Wilcox, Jr., who is the dispatcher for St. Lawrence Freightways. "She knows how to handle a tractor and trailer and she has a good reputation."

Muriel and Ken Hayes transport products such as printing paper, talc, venetian blinds, and dry milk whey from local manufacturers to their consignees in an area extending from Buffalo and Rochester to New York City, New Jersey, and Long Island.

Muriel's husband likes having her drive. "We get to see each more often this way," he says. "The company tries to send us in

Muriel Hayes, waitress turned owner-operator

the same general direction and to give us the same days off."

Muriel admits to having been interested in trucking in her younger days when she was a tomboy growing up in Springfield, Vermont, but she never had an opportunity to learn to drive a truck until her husband taught her about eight years ago. Now she thoroughly enjoys her work. "It's interesting. It pays every week, and I like to meet people and go places." Since she and her husband operate their own trucking firm, K & M Enterprises, on weekends, chances are she will be trucking for a long time to come.

Not all lady drivers are in partnership with their husbands. Take "Grandma Hemlock." Her real name is Donna John. She's five-foot-two with eyes of blue, and she drives a powder blue and black Mack Western RL 767 LST. She herself enameled her trailer to match the tractor. To complete her coordinated appearance with her rig, she wears a powder blue hard hat.

Donna is a gypo logger. (A gypo is an independent driver who leases her truck to whoever will give her a load to carry.) She gets paid on percentage, scale, ton, or trip. This personable little grandma handles her logging truck as well as any of the men. She needs help from no one when she throws the heavy wrappers over a load of logs three times her height and pulls the binders down to secure her load. She works shoulder to shoulder with men more than twice her size. Yet she makes as many loads each day as the best of them.

Donna's mechanical knowledge is almost inborn. Her father, a logger, rancher, and fleet owner, taught her to handle every piece of farm machinery they had just as soon as her feet could reach the pedals.

What prompted her to become a gypo logger? She has five

Karen Vecchio enjoys her man-sized job driving for Joseph Chiappone Lime Spreading.

*Testing the glad hands . . .
checking the tires . . .
dumping the load. There's
more to trucking than holding the steering wheel.*

children to raise. "The money is pretty good for a woman," she says. "It's long hours and hard work. On weekends the truck needs washing and servicing, but I enjoy logging."

Donna is willing to talk about her profession, but she gets tired of being pointed out as one of the few women log-truck drivers. "I'm not a women's libber," she says, "but if it will help other women to do what they want to do, I'll carry a sign for equal opportunity till the cows come home."

It's possible to work your way up from a smaller truck to a semi if that's your goal. Karen Vecchio aspires to do just that. Right now climbing atop a ten-wheeled lime spreader is all in a day's work for this twenty-one-year-old driver from Watertown, New York. When the lime she is spreading for a customer cakes in the spreader, it's up to her to climb up and shovel it loose.

Karen got her Class III license and began driving when she was twenty at a salary of five dollars an hour. She enjoys driving and hopes to earn her Class I license in the near future. The experience she is getting right now will certainly be a help to her when she takes on the responsibilities of eight more wheels.

Many ladies find satisfaction in jobs that are essential to keeping trucks on the road. (In a later chapter you'll read about these jobs in detail.) A few women have already established themselves firmly in the industry because they have proved themselves competent and efficient in handling jobs formerly entrusted to men.

Bernice MacDonald's trucking career began during World War II, when she left North Central College to help out her father who owned a trucking business but had lost many of his drivers to the armed forces. She continued driving for twenty-eight years until November, 1976, when she "retired" from behind the wheel to take up her new duties as full-time teacher and the lead instructor for the night shift at Fox Valley Technical Institute.

Bernice is well qualified for her job of teaching truck driving. During her years on the highway she never had an accident. For this outstanding record she earned the top award from the Amer-

Ladies who have a mechanical interest and inclination can find satisfying employment helping assemble the big tractors.

Computerization speeds up the trucking industry and provides many job opportunities for those who are trained in this field of operation.

Instructor Bernice Mac-
Donald of the Fox Valley
Technical Institute (Wiscon-
sin) demonstrates a point to
students Mary Bergman and
Steven Bartels.

Wanda Ellis, administrative
manager, chats with owner-
operator, Bob Decker. Bob
began driving when he was
seventeen. His load here is
long sections of plastic pipe.

ican Trucking Associations. Mack Trucks, Inc. awarded her their Million Mile Award in recognition of her driving record. Both the Wisconsin Motor Carriers Association and the Wisconsin Transportation Company publicly recognized her outstanding record as a trucker.

Bernice can recall incidences when after she had pulled in to a truck stop for coffee, a few drivers would run outside to see if she had hit their rigs in the process. Those days were long ago, but the remembrance of them makes her all the more determined to teach her students as carefully as her father taught her.

Wanda Ellis, Administrative Manager for Specialized Commodities, Flatbed Division, Arkansas-Best Freight System, Inc., was originally a part-time worker at ABF. Then she became a payroll clerk, and then secretary to the vice president. She worked for a time as dispatcher before assuming her current position. Wanda's experiences with ABF are proof that a qualified lady can work her way up in the trucking industry.

Lesley Simeral is one of the few female truck salespersons in the United States. Since 1974 she has been employed at North-

Lesley Simeral began her trucking career selling International Scouts. Here she demonstrates an International Fleetstar medium-heavy-duty truck at Northside International.

side International, about twenty miles northwest of Chicago.

Lesley studied at Bradley University and the Chicago Academy of Fine Arts, but then decided against a career in interior design. Her younger brother, who was employed at International Harvester in Chicago, suggested she try truck sales.

Jerry Nottoli, president of Northside International, was not enthusiastic about hiring a woman for a sales position, but he consented to an interview with Lesley.

"She handled herself extremely well," recalls Nottoli. "She used salesmanship. At least three different times she asked for the job in different ways. I knew she wanted the job and would not leave without a definite answer. I decided that if she could sell trucks as well, she would be a success."

Nottoli was impressed with Lesley's qualifications. He also holds the belief that today's truck market is not entirely a man's world.

"A truck purchase, particularly a Scout or light-duty model, often is a family decision. If a salesperson can understand and empathize with what's going on in the customer's mind, we're that much closer to a successful sale," he says.

Lesley sold her first Scout on her third day at work, and she has continued to be successful. She's careful about her personal appearance, and she places a great premium on product knowledge and enthusiasm in selling. She studies to increase her understanding of her work, and she is a twenty-four-hour-a-day fan of the International Scout she drives as her regular transportation. Jerry Nottoli has not regretted the day he hired such a determined and capable young salesperson.

Elizabeth "Liz" Gray, an attractive widow and mother of four boys, has dealt with truck buyers and parts and service people for more than ten years. She is currently heavy-duty advertising coordinator for the Ford Division of Ford Motor Company.

Liz is a graduate of Penn State with a Bachelor of Arts degree in liberal arts. She became interested in heavy-duty truck merchandising during the ten years she worked for Mack Trucks as marketing communications manager. Writing in *Open Road*, she

Liz Gray, heavy-duty truck advertising coordinator for Ford, is a marketing specialist with a decade of experience in communicating with those who purchase the big rigs.

states, "The challenge we in heavy-duty truck advertising face is to present a total buying picture. We stress the message that quality starts with a dependable, tough, and classy rig that will enable the buyer to make a profit."

According to Liz, there are few women in the heavy-duty merchandising field because women haven't tried to enter. She insists that men are glad to give the ladies a chance in fields that are relatively new to them.

Because of her years of experience at Mack, Liz understands the language of the fleet truck buyers as well as the owner-operators. That's what makes her a success.

10

TRUCKING CAREERS OTHER THAN DRIVING

The trucking industry provides direct employment for more than nine million people. That's one in every ten persons employed in the United States. Approximately 850,000 of these employees are truck drivers. The others hold a variety of jobs. Thousands are employed in truck body and trailer manufacturing, vehicle sales and service, fuel production, and highway con-

Thousands of workers per-
form a variety of jobs in as-
sembling a tractor from
retouching the paint (opposite page) to making the
final inspection at the end of
the assembly line.

Gold-leafing a fire company's insignia and number is a highly specialized skill. Artists hand-paint each insignia on the door.

Besides pay and benefits, the real reward in putting together a big rig
is the thrill in watching it roll off the assembly line.

Before the assembly line rolls, parts must be manufactured. Women can find job opportunities in parts plants. This lady displays sand molds for castings at the International Truck Engine Plant in Indianapolis.

Many behind-the-scenes workers help produce a truck. Here a technician operates a solid-state programmable controller to produce truck engine moldings.

struction and maintenance. Others work as lawyers, accountants, maintenance men, and computer personnel.

Trucking companies hire personnel to work in areas such as sales; freight movement; claims, safety, and insurance; data processing (rates and billing as well as accounting); maintenance; and management and administration. They may also employ medical doctors and nurses.

Manufacturing companies hire assembly-line workers, machine operators, scientists, test drivers, and tool and die makers. Terminals have a work force comprised of mechanics, safety experts, freight handlers, and record keepers.

The trucking industry employs persons with varied amounts of education. Your choice of a career will depend upon the amount of training you are willing to get. Some truck-related jobs, like factory-skilled craftsman and mechanic, do not require a college degree.

If you are proficient in touch typing, accounting, or some form of data processing, you are qualified for many of the clerical jobs in the trucking field. If you want a job in management, you will need to pursue a college degree. Many companies will provide on-the-job training, beginning with the skills the employee already has.

You can secure a list of colleges offering degrees in transpor-

About one out of eight employees in the trucking industry has a clerical job.

tation by writing for the "Directory of Transportation Education," Education Section, ATA, 1616 P Street, Washington, D.C. 20036.

About one out of every eight of the workers in the trucking industry has a clerical job. Many are of a general nature like secretary or clerk-typist, such as you would find in any industry. Others have specialized jobs, such as dispatchers, rate clerks, claims clerks, manifest clerks, and parts order clerks.

To qualify for a clerical job, you should take a commercial course in high school or attend business school. You will need additional on-the-job training for the specialized clerical occupations such as rate or claims clerk.

The Ford Motor Company, in cooperation with the American Trucking Associations, Inc., has printed an informative brochure with illustrated job descriptions. Here's the way they describe the job opportunities in trucking.

SALES

First, sales. The salesman must show the prospective customer he can get the freight there faster, better, and more safely than other companies. His job is to help his customers solve their physical distribution problems. It is essential that he know his client's special needs as well as his manufacturing and marketing methods. For example, is the goods perishable, odd-shaped, or in need of some special conditions for transporting?

To prepare for this job, the salesman acquires a thorough knowledge of his company's freight rates, the routes of his line-haul trucks, the minimum hauling times between major points, and special trailers or equipment available for special loads. If a customer asks how long it will take to deliver a load to Cleveland, he can't say, "Wait a minute. I'll look it up." He must know right then, if he wants to gain this customer's next load.

Once he has gained the customer's business, the salesman must follow through on the freight, making good on the promised service so he can insure future good relations and hopefully more business from the same client.

Lesley Simeral, truck salesperson for International Trucks, calls a potential customer.

A background in business, such as is offered in a two-year training program, would be a real asset to the salesman. If he has plenty of initiative, he can move up to regional sales manager, to company sales manager, and even into top management.

FREIGHT MOVEMENT

A large trucking terminal may have sixty to eighty bays (loading docks) at which trucks are docked for loading and unloading. In order to give fast, efficient service, the terminal operates twenty-four hours a day. As soon as a trailer is loaded, a linehaul tractor moves out with it on its designated route, and an empty trailer is moved into its place. Hundreds of different freight consignments may move in and out of the terminal every day. Each piece has to be recorded and loaded into a truck scheduled for the right destination. In addition to the city driver or the linehaul driver who picks up the freight to carry it to its destination, there are three other groups of workers involved in freight movement.

Freight must be loaded safely and according to a plan.

Furniture must be wrapped to protect it from scratches in transit.

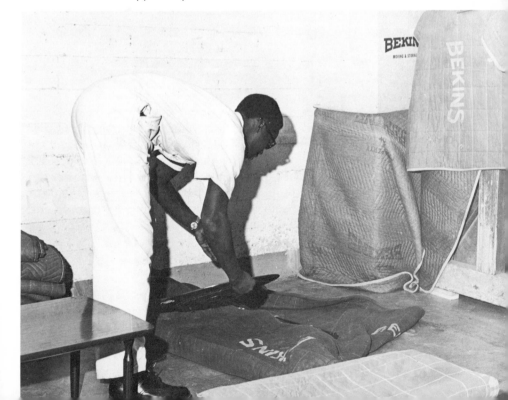

They are the dock workers, the dispatcher, and the terminal manager.

Dock workers have various titles. These include materials handlers, dock foreman or forewoman, gang leader, dock supervisor, power truck operators, crane operators, and truck driver's helper. The job of these employees is to load the freight swiftly and safely, being certain to load first the freight that will be unloaded last.

Dock workers must be strong physically. They must also be careful, responsible workers who do not damage the freight they are handling. The work is hard, but a job on the dock has often been the first step up the ladder to a good career in the trucking industry.

The dispatcher coordinates trucks and goods in and out of the terminal. He makes up the loads for specific destinations, and assigns the drivers delivery schedules. He also handles the customers' requests for freight pick-up. He sees that drivers have the right freight bills to deliver their goods. He uses a telephone, a teletype, and a radio intercom to keep track of every truck and driver on the road. Many dispatchers work their way up to the job from dock worker, to dock supervisor, to dispatcher.

The terminal manager plans and directs all freight operations. He supervises the operation of the truck terminal. He is responsible for safety considerations, accounting, and labor relations at his terminal. His salary reflects his great responsibilities.

CLAIMS/SAFETY/INSURANCE

When goods does not arrive, or when it arrives damaged, the owner makes a claim against the trucking company. This claim must be settled quickly and fairly to insure good relationships between the two companies involved.

The claims adjuster traces the shipment to find out where the responsibility for the damage or the delay lies. Then he works out a fair settlement. He must know freight rates and commodity values to do this job.

The safety director supervises a program to keep vehicles in safe operating condition, to keep all areas accident-free, and to prevent accidents on the road. He investigates every accident with the help of his associates in radio-equipped cars that constantly patrol the carrier's route.

Millions of dollars' worth of equipment and freight on the move each day must be protected by insurance. Trucking employees have to be covered, and customers must be protected against damage and/or loss. Thus the insurance officer needs a thorough knowledge of federal and state regulations relative to insurance protection. He needs a broad familiarity with insurance as it applies to truck transportation. His position is an important one; his right decisions can save his company money.

Other jobs in this area include the claims clerk, the assistant insurance manager, safety supervisors, the assistant safety director, and the driver trainer.

DATA PROCESSING/RATES AND BILLING/ACCOUNTING

The trucking industry has experienced a revolution in speed, accuracy, cost control, and general efficiency due to the adoption of ultra modern computer systems. Dispatching, rate analysis, billing, accounting, payroll, taxes, and company communications in general are now handled through electronic circuits. In mere seconds telecommunications can bring information as to the status and whereabouts of any truck, trailer, or driver in the company's entire system of terminals—with facts about load, load weight, destination, scheduled arrival, and time in the maintenance shop.

If data processing interests you, you would be wise to take any courses available in that field that your high school or college offers. Many trucking companies are equipped to train new employees right on the job, but you'll have a head start if you come with some background. If you can type, that will help you learn to use the keypunch or computer.

The variety of jobs in this category include junior rate clerk, rate clerk, auditor, accountant, accountants' supervisor, accounting manager, general accounting manager, systems analyst, computer operator, and keypunch clerk. Like many areas of the industry, data processing offers the opportunity to work yourself up into a job with more responsibilities and a larger salary.

MAINTENANCE AND REPAIR

The job of the maintenance department of a carrier is to see that both tractors and trailers are serviced and ready to roll at any time. Preventative maintenance—catching trouble before it starts—is an important part of the job.

Mechanics, parts clerks, and shop foremen work under the director of maintenance to keep the equipment in shape so it won't break down. Down time on the road, due to breakdowns, or holdups in the terminal for repairs are costly to the company and hurt customer relations.

Large terminals that operate on a twenty-four-hour-a-day schedule have dozens of mechanics working in three shifts.

Preventative maintenance is most important, so routine checks are made on each vehicle.

Qualified mechanics can reduce down time for a driver and his rig.

These "hood lifters" check every truck carefully after each trip out, even if it has been a very short one. They use a checklist which covers everything from safety equipment, like fire extinguishers, to windshield wipers, and the depth of the tire tread. The drivers of the trucks must report on a routine form any equipment problems they have had on the road that might require special attention.

One of the devices used to test equipment to spot engine wear and defective parts is a *dynamometer*. This machine simulates highway conditions while the truck is standing still in the shop. It gives a quick, accurate check on the engine's performance.

Maintenance personnel include the parts clerk, the service garage worker, the lubrication person and washer, mechanics helpers, apprentice mechanics, journeyman mechanics, shop foreman, shop supervisor, and the director of equipment and maintenance.

J. B. Grant, supervisor of the International Truck Training Institute at Atlanta, demonstrates the use of a dynamometer for testing an International DT-466 diesel engine.

The National Institute for Automotive Excellence, with headquarters in Washington, D.C., has a training program for certifying heavy-duty truck mechanics.

MANAGEMENT AND ADMINISTRATION

Because the trucking business is growing so fast, it needs administrators and managers faster than they can be found. A shortage of good people at the management level can be damaging to a company. That's why an increasing number of companies have their own management training programs and actively recruit trainees at the college level.

A capable young person can be realistic and still plan to become the owner of a company. There are many possibilities because there are so many trucking companies. The great changes in trucking due to computerization and more sophisticated com-

W. W. Johnson (left), marketing consultant, looks over used truck marketing statistics with T. E. Reimers (center), fleet sales manager, and W. E. Keehan, used truck manager.

Robert Ross (left), Richmond, Indiana, became an International Truck dealer in 1974. He is touring IH quality control center at Indianapolis with plant manager, Rodney W. Dunham.

pany systems offer the young manager/administrator many opportunities to be creative and innovative.

If management is your goal, you should pursue a college career in areas such as business administration, accounting, or transportation. There is plenty of room at the top for the qualified person who is willing to work.

A PHOTOGRAPHIC ESSAY OF A TRUCK TRAINING CENTER

International Harvester's Truck Division operates five regional Truck Training Centers. Each center offers a number of comprehensive programs for truck servicemen, as well as training in sales, administration and management, and dealer personnel. Regular class sessions are held for four full days. Subjects covered in this concentrated study program include engine tune-up for both diesel and gasoline power plants, air conditioning, transmissions, noise abatement, carburetion, driveline, diesel pump, exhaust emission, and the new DOT (Department of Transportation) brake program.

The International Harvester training program is a tuition-free service for all IH branches, dealers, and fleet customers. The centers operate eleven months a year, enabling dealers and fleets to send their servicemen to various courses on a continuous basis. New courses are constantly being developed to meet the new technical innovations as they develop.

The following photographs are from the training center at San Leandro, California. Other centers are located in Dallas, Chicago, Atlanta, and Baltimore.

International truck dealers and fleet customer service personel study diesel engine tune-up troubleshooting and noise abatement.

Troubleshooting a truck air conditioning system is part of the learning-by-doing instruction program.

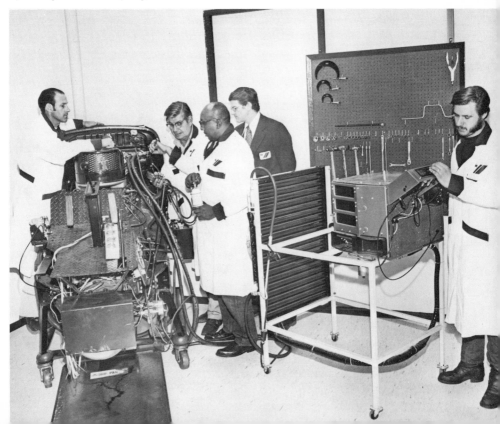

Each student is given his own carburetor to work on for a course in emission engine carburetion and ignition diagnostic procedures.

Right: Principles of Federal Motor Vehicle Safety Standard 121 air brakes are explained on this special display that combines all components on an operational brake board.

Students test an IH gasoline engine for exhaust emission with the help of an electronic diagnostic control monitor.

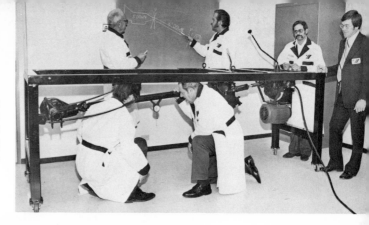

How to determine proper specification for driveline angle is the problem being considered here.

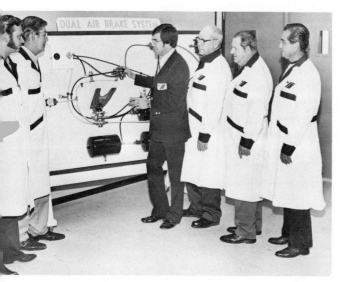

Below: "Driving with DOT Air Brakes," a new "SuperCom" audio-visual training program, familarizes drivers with the FMVSS 121 air brakes.

THE TOTAL PICTURE

According to the U.S. Department of Labor, employment in the trucking industry is expected to grow rapidly through the mid-1980s. Job openings will be created by employment growth as well as by vacancies due to retirement, death, or transfer to other occupations.

Employment will not increase as fast as the demand for trucking services. This is because technological developments and the trend toward larger, more efficient firms will increase output per worker.

Rates of growth will vary among occupations. For example, employment of materials handlers will increase slowly because of more efficient freight-handling methods such as conveyors and drag lines to move freight in and out of terminals and warehouses. More and more cargo will be put into metal cages when there is less than a truck load to be picked up. These cages, which are really large wire boxes, can be picked up much faster than many smaller boxes.

Because of the trend toward larger companies, accountants, personnel workers, clerks, sales workers, and truck mechanics will be in greater demand. The need for terminal managers will decrease, since they do many tasks that are assigned to other workers in larger companies.

No matter what your interest is in the trucking industry, you can find a job you like if you plan ahead and prepare carefully for it.

11

TRUCKERS HAVE FUN

Many truck drivers enjoy their work so much on the road that even in their leisure time they choose activities related to their jobs. They have CB radios in their homes as well as in their rigs. Whether on the road or off, they continue the constant communion they share with other truckers as they keep their sets tuned to Channel 19, the truckers' channel.

Some truckers who first became acquainted by CB radio have the pleasure of meeting face-to-face at truckers' conventions. These gatherings are held annually throughout the United States and Canada. They range in size from local mini-shows which attract a few hundred people to international expositions featuring gigantic displays of mammoth trucks and related equipment, with attendance in the thousands.

The exhibits at the shows are geared to showing the trucker and his family what products are new, how they work, and where they can be purchased. The shows offer an opportunity to talk face-to-face with manufacturers and sales personnel who are experts in every phase of trucking. There are seminars, panel dis-

ARIE CROWN THEATRE

TRUCK WEEK '76 COUNTRY WESTERN NITE STARRING CHARLIE R
& FEATURING 2ND ANNUAL TRUCK DRIVERS' COUNTRY MUSIC AW

Charlie Rich, a favorite among truckers, presides at the second annual Truck Drivers' Country Music Awards in 1976.

cussions, forums, and addresses by people knowledgeable in the trucking industry.

Additional entertainment is provided in the form of banquets, dances, games, movies, skills contests, and drawings for prizes. There is much time for socializing.

The largest conventions are designed for the tractor trailer drivers, but all are welcome to attend, whether they are truckers or not. The big exhibitions include the International Trucking Show which has both an East and West Division, the Mid-America Trucking Show held in Louisville, the New England Truck and Truck Equipment Show in Boston, which is believed to attract the highest percentage of "real" truckers, the Truckers Convention sponsored by *Overdrive* magazine, the Truckers Jamboree and Expo held by Radio Station WWVA in Wheeling, West Virginia, Truck Week, the Big "I" in Chicago, and the National Trucker's Convention.

Truckers who live or haul in Canada have their choice of several conventions as well. These include the Canadian National Truck and Equipment Exhibition, the National Canadian Trucking Convention and Exhibition, the Canadian Trucking Industry Trade Show, and Truckers' Days.

A highlight of Truck Week is the annual Truck Drivers' Country Music Awards show. Charlie Rich, a favorite vocalist among truckers, and Charlie Douglas, the truckers' favorite DJ from Radio Station WWL, New Orleans, have presided over these shows since their inception in the mid-1970s. The winners are chosen previously by ballot, and they are presented truck trophies accompanied by the enthusiastic applause of the trucking audience.

One of the newer trucking events is the Northeast Regional Trucker's Fair and CB Jamboree. The first one was held in Allentown, Pennsylvania, in 1976, and attracted over 60,000 truckers, CBers, and country music fans from as far away as Anchorage, Alaska. The jamboree featured displays of trucking and CB equipment, contests for attenders, and a big rig beauty competition.

TRUCK RACING

Truckers' drag races? That's right. Racing is a popular sport in the United States, and the big rigs have gotten in on it, too. Several big events were held for driving and racing fans in 1976. More than 6,000 spectators and contestants thrilled when Ron Anderson of Lexington, Illinois, carried off the "Top Eliminator" title at the Nationals at Indianapolis Raceway Park. Ron was teaming a Detroit diesel-powered Peterbilt.

"Transtar Rose," Ms. Bonnie
Nelson

At the races at Ontario Motor Speedway in Ontario, California, twenty-year-old Jim Kinkle, from Chatsworth, proved himself "King of the Hill." Jim raced a mean 1953 Kenworth powered by a 220 blown Cummins with 263 horsepower.

Down in Texas the Lone Star Big Rig Truck Race and Roadeo Championship featured a 300-foot dash for "freight jockeys," a timed docking test, and a quarter-mile speed trial from a standing start. Jerry "Tyrone" Malone and his Super Boss were a big hit at this event. Tyrone's snorting 1,000 hp of diesel dynamite set a world's record of 100.55 mph at this race held in Smithfield. The Super Boss has since broken its own record. At Bonneville, with Bill Snyder, Thermo King's marketing vice president, at the wheel, it was clocked at 144.381 on the first leg, and 144.462 on the return for an average of 144.21 mph.

As one would expect, this racy Super Boss is a special attraction at drag races wherever it is present. It is a 1974 Kenworth wide-nosed, two-axle, conventional tractor. Tyrone designed and built it at a cost of $150,000. An interesting and innovative safety feature on this mighty monster is the skis. They are mounted under the front springs below the rim level to maintain control should a front tire blow in a high-speed run. The truck also has a two-inch tubular full roll cage in the cab.

Drag races continue to be held throughout the country. Prizes are offered in many classes of working diesels and sometimes for modified trucks, exhibition-type trucks, and even for diesel-powered pickups.

Though not a drag race, the annual roadeo held by the State-wide Towing Association of Massachusetts at the Three County Fairgrounds in Northampton each fall has featured a unique trucking event, a wrecker race. The event is held to see which tow truck can upright a "wrecked" double-bottom rig in the shortest time.

Many trucking families enjoy the Transtar Rose American Road Show. This is a country-and-western musical production that tours the country for about three months each year. It is sponsored by International Harvester's Truck Division and features Ms. Bonnie Nelson, "Transtar Rose." The show is presented nightly at truck stops and at International truck dealerships and service centers. The public is invited to attend free of charge. Your local IH dealer can tell you when there will be a show in your area.

By reading trucking magazines and visiting truck stops, you can find out the dates for the trucking events near where you live. Most of these exhibitions welcome anyone who has an interest in trucks. Many have no admission charges. If you are really interested in trucking, you should attend as many trucking events as you can. You will be able to rub shoulders with real truckers. Next to hopping into the cab with a driver, this is the best place to find out about the trucking industry.

12

TRUCKING HOBBIES

If you really love trucks and just can't wait until you're old enough to drive, there are some interesting things you can do right now to keep yourself in tune with the truckers' world. How much you get involved depends upon the amount of time and money you wish to spend.

We mentioned earlier the importance of the CB radio to the truck driver. If you tune your set to Channel 19, or whatever channel the truckers in your vicinity use, you can listen in or talk with drivers any hour of the day or night. You'll find the conversation entertaining as well as instructive. Most drivers will talk with you when you tell them you hope to become a gearjammer too.

Your AM radio will keep you in touch with truckers' songs. Nearly every station in the country played C. W. McCall's "Convoy" until the record must have been worn smooth. And there have been other trucking songs that have made their way up the charts, such as "Tombstone Every Mile," "White Knight," and "Phantom 309."

Depending upon where you live, you may be able to tune in an all-night radio station which gears its programming to truckers from midnight on.

One of the most popular of all DJs with truckers is Charlie Douglas, who operates out of WWL, New Orleans, at 870 on the dial. Other DJs whom the teamsters like because they program for them include Jack Reno, WLW, Cincinnati, at 700; Chuck Sullivan from KLAC, Los Angeles, at 570; and Larry James, heard over WBT, Charlotte, at 1110.

During the 1970s at least four movies were produced with truck drivers as heroes. Their creation may have been due in part to the interest generated by the now defunct "Movin' On" television series. Though not always protraying the trucking scene accurately, the series did stir up interest in the important part trucks play in our transportation network. *White Line Fever* was the first of the feature-length trucking films. It was followed by *Moonfire*, the adult comedy *Smokey and the Bandit*, and *Citizens Band*, which features a truck driver (Chuck Napier) in a starring role.

TRUCKING GAMES

Table games are a fun way for the entire family to participate in some trucking experiences. A number of board games are

The entire family can enjoy trucking games like *Over the Road*.

available in hobby shops and department stores to give you and your friends an idea of what it's like to team a big rig.

In Over the Road (Anmar Games, Inc.) you pick a route and travel on major interstate highways across the United States. With Parker Brothers' game, 10-Four, Good Buddy, each player is a trucker equipped with CB cards which give highway directions. Breaker 19, the CB Truckers Game (Milton Bradley Company) challenges the players to be the first to make a payment on their rigs. That's Trucking (Showker, Inc.) also puts the player in the driver's seat.

MAGAZINES

A number of trucking magazines are published on a regular schedule. Some are designed for specific audiences such as fleet owners, "reefer" drivers, or cattle haulers. Others are published for a general audience of truckers. If you are just getting interested in trucking, you would enjoy reading *Open Road and the Professional Driver*. This monthly gives a rather broad picture of what is relevant to the truck driver. It tells what is going on in Washington, how to care for your equipment, and what other truckers are doing and thinking. It is well illustrated and covers

The Mack Shop at Allentown, Pennsylvania, offers a generous selection of Mack items for sale.

subjects of interest to the driver's family as well.

Two magazines that continue the personal element but are more technical are *Heavy Duty Trucking* and *Owner Operator.* If you are most interested in the independent owner-operator and what affects him, you should read *Overdrive.* However, this is an expensive magazine with much "cheesecake." The magazine does give lots of detailed photographs and illustrations of new trucks and trucking equipment.

If you are interested in truck-related items such as stationery, belt buckles, jewelry, hats, shirts, and so on, you will find them advertised in the trucking magazines. You can also find them for sale in the larger truck stops and at plants where trucks are manufactured.

Giant, full-color posters can be purchased from the Power Graphics Corporation, P.O. Box 817, Denville, New Jersey 07834.

BUILDING SCALE MODELS

If you are nimble-fingered and like to build things, you can have a lot of fun constructing scale models of trucks and trailers. The standard sizes are 1/25 and 1/43. There are smaller ones on the market, such as 1/87, but they have much less detail.

Two companies that do an outstanding job of producing kits are the Ertl Company and AMT. Ertl Blueprint Replica plastic models are designed and documented with the original manufacturer's blueprints. Every kit comes with a detailed instruction manual showing step-by-step construction details. Each step is illustrated with clear line drawings and photographs of model construction, as well as painting and super-detailing instructions.

AMT produces an extensive line of over-the-road trucks and trailers, also scaled from the manufacturer's official blueprints. Some modelers feel the instructions are not quite as clear in these kits, though they are carefully prepared.

Big Rigs were introduced in the fall of 1977. Big Rigs kits come in a series of three individual vehicles plus two tandem combinations, each presented in a full-color package that il-

It takes time, patience, and some basic tools to build a model like this Mack DM-600 truck dump trailer.

A "Blueprint Replica" model of the Transtar II "Eagle" Cabover

The Big Rig truck line

lustrates the vehicles in a suggested paint scheme. Each box panel lists the additional, suggested, and optional tools and materials recommended to achieve a professionally finished model. Another panel provides interesting detail photographs about the specific model in the package. Big Rigs are manufactured by the Testor Corporation.

Kits produced by Ertl and AMT, as well as by other companies, can be bought at hobby stores, discount houses, and in many retail store outlets. If you can't find a specific model in your local shop, you can write directly to the company to see if it is available. The address is on the box of each kit.

After you have assembled a few trucks and trailers according to the directions that accompany each kit, you may become venturesome and begin to adapt kits to conform to trucks you have seen on the road or that you have dreamed up in your imagination. Auto World, 701 N. Keyser Avenue, Scranton, Pennsylvania 18505, specializes in models and supplies. For a modest fee this company will send you their catalog listing models and accessories from more than two hundred different companies. Besides listing products available, the catalog contains many detailed, helpful hints and suggestions for building models.

In addition to Auto World, you can purchase supplies from William K. Walthers, Inc., 5601 Florist Avenue, Milwaukee,

Building model trucks is a hobby enjoyed by many. However, it's a good idea to have an experienced modeler help you with your first one.

Wisconsin 53218. This company specializes in HO railroad supplies, but it also sells model trucks and items that the creative modeler will need to adapt a kit to his own personal design.

You can get help in learning to build your own models by subscribing to the Ertl *Blueprinter*, which is an illustrated quarterly containing notes, news, and helps for the model builder.

At least three model builders have gained a name for themselves because of their skill in construction. One of these is Lou Kroack who edits a monthly detailed feature in *Owner Operator* called "Table Top Trucking." Each month he brings his readers up to date on what's new in modeling by giving specific information and illustrations. Then he lists two winners in his Truckarama contest. To enter this competition, you send him one or two sharp, clear, black and white photographs of your model. In addition to the fun of seeing a picture of your model in print, if you are the winner, you also earn some worthwhile prizes.

Overdrive includes in its pages photographs of its "Model of the Month," so you can also enter a photograph of your model in this magazine competition.

Both AMT and Auto World sponsor contests for modelers. AMT offers prizes to builders who have used their own kits, whereas Auto World seeks original ideas for building, painting, or decorating trucks made from any model kit.

Phil Jensen is another well-known modeler. He shares his expertise in a book entitled *Building Model Trucks* (Haessner Publishing Company, Newfoundland, New Jersey 07435). You'll find this book most helpful if you are a serious modeler.

The greatest model builder of all must be James E. Etter. Jim is a professional model-maker who heads up American Industrial Models, McConnellsburg, Pennsylvania 17233. He offers his custom-built, made-to-order conversion kits for sale to expert modelers who are ready for a real challenge. You can keep up to date with Jim's products by reading Lou Kroack's column in *Owner Operator* each month.

Some companies, such as Lindberg, manufacture plastic kits that snap together. They require much less manipulative skill than the 1/25 scale models that must be glued together. One

Jim Etter's custom-built Crane Carrier "Centurion" COE

thing is certain. You will gain a lot of know-how if you put together very many models. That would be a fun way to learn more about trucking.

However, if your middle name is "Fumble Fingers," you'd better forget the model building. You can concentrate on collecting miniatures and scale-model trucks. Check your local hobby shops and read the back pages of trucking magazines to find new models to add to your collection.

13

TOMORROW'S TRUCKS

To understand futuristic-designed trucks, you must know the term *aerodynamics*. Aerodynamics is the study of the relationship between motion and the forces of the atmosphere which affect motion. Designers of tomorrow's trucks feel that aerodynamics will play a key role because the name of the game is fuel efficiency.

Since the mid-1970s truck designers have been working out devices and designs to streamline their products and save fuel. Roof-mounted wind deflectors with or without vortex stabilizers, gap seals between cab and trailer, thermatic fans, radial tires, higher axle ratios, and lighter materials were introduced to reduce air drag and to permit trucks to operate more economically.

Michael Lamm, West Coast editor for *Popular Mechanics*, feels that tomorrow's trucks will go even further into streamlining. He sees today's boxy shapes giving way to some laid-back profiles with rounder corners. He also points out that such sweeping changes will come slowly because of the extremely high costs of tooling radical new designs.

This aerodynamic rig's innovative features include a two-piece curved windshield, side-mounted radiators, and rectangular headlights.

Larry Shinoda, one of America's top truck designers, in an interview with *Owner Operator*, also recognized the importance of aerodynamic design. He agreed that drastic changes in design will not come immediately *unless* the government mandates that trucks produce a certain miles-per-gallon figure.

According to Shinoda, truck designers will look for things that make trucking cheaper and more profitable for the operator—things like cab suspension, better driving comfort, and ease of maintenance.

Shinoda's schematic designs *could* be constructed, but chances are they will not be. He says he uses them as "provokers." They include a race car type of fuel tank which has a fuel bladder, side-mounted radiators or heat exchangers, rectangular headlights, flush marker lights that can be seen from the side or the front, and a type of electrically charged device on the windshield that makes wipers unnecessary. The driver will know what's behind him through a closed-circuit television system. These are designs

Trailers like these could carry both liquid and dry freight at the same time. Many fleets would find this arrangement an advantage. Actually, the concept is not too different from caging cargo, which is becoming more and more widespread.

that *could* be built. The future will dictate if they will be.

NASA has been experimenting with trucks and vans since 1974. Their researchers have discovered that the most common wind deflector cuts drag up to 24 percent at 55 mph. They also revealed that cutting the gap between the tractor and the trailer from the normal 62-inch to 64-inch spacing to 40 inches reduced drag up to 19 percent.

NASA added aluminum exterior skins to a test box trailer with 90° corners. By rounding the corners and sealing the underbody with a three-quarter-length bellypan, they reduced drag to 61 percent. We can't conclude from these tests that all dragfoilers, rounded corners, and bellypans work equally well under all conditions, but the tests do show the value of continued study in this area.

Innovative designs are not just on the drawing boards. In 1976, *Heavy Duty Trucking* reported on a Ryder tractor, one of ten prototypes produced by the Hendrickson Manufacturing Company, with an aerodynamic design. The trucks were reported to have represented a 25 percent fuel saving. It was said that the fuel-saving devices, which included a wind deflector, radial tires, thermatic fan, and fuel efficient engine, would pay for themselves within six months or less of highway use.

Strick, Inc., trailer manufacturers in Ft. Washington, Pennsylvania, has designed a nose-cone trailer to maximize the carrying capacity of the largest legal tractor trailer combination.

In this new design, Strick has lengthened and lowered the trailer and tucked a small, streamlined, one-man tractor under the leading edge. The driver sits at about the same height as he would in a conventional car. The trailer pivots atop the cab roof. The concept was originally proposed with four-wheel steering, high-flotation single tires, and up to 80,000 GVW (Gross Vehicle Weight). This vehicle emphasizes cargo capacity first and streamlining second.

In 1977 the New York Telephone Company put into service in New York City five nonpolluting, energy-saving, and virtually noiseless battery-powered vehicles, called Electrucks. The trucks cost $6,000 each and were powered by a 54-volt, 1,300-pound

Strick's cab-under tractor would maximize carrying capacity.

Tomorrow's truckers

battery. They were used as part of the company's coin-telephone repair fleet.

According to designer Shinoda, "How tomorrow's trucks will actually look depends on customer demand, government regulations, and technological advances."

If you have a scientific interest in new design, you would do well to study engineering and/or drafting. Then look for a job in the test and research development department of one of the major trucking companies. You'll find the work challenging and rewarding, with only the sky as the limit to what you might dream up. Who knows? *You* might become the Henry Ford of the twenty-first century!

INDEX

Accidents, 11–13, 92–93, 108–110
Advance United Expressway, 121
Advice to prospective drivers, 65, 67, 74, 82, 84, 130
Aerodynamics, 17, 19, 42–43, 173–174
Age qualifications, driving, 76
Air brakes, 57–58, 156–157. *See also* 121 brakes
Air conditioning, 155 Mark IV, 29
Air starter, 45
Airfoil. *See* Wind deflector
Allentown, Pennsylvania, 161, 166
Alternator. *See* Charging system
American Trucking Associations, Inc., 84, 100, 109, 113, 137, 145
Anchorage, Alaska, 161
Anderson, Ron, 161
Anmar Games, Inc., 166
Apollo Truck Brokerage, 84
Arskansas-Best Freight Systems, Inc., 137
Atherton, Geri, 111
Atlanta, Georgia, 152, 154

Aubin, Armand E., Jr., 10–13
Aucter, John, 65–67
Auto World, 169
Autocar trucks, 25, 35
Awards
    Driver of the Month, 108
    Driver of the Year, 108–110
    Maintenance Man of the Year, 112
    Million Mile Award, 137
    Queen of the Road, 110–112
    Truck Drivers' Country Music Awards, 160–161
    See also Medals
Axle, 15, 54

Bagwell, Eileen, 112
Baltimore, Maryland, 154
Bartels, Steven, 136
Bedford, Indiana, 122
Bekins Van Lines Company, 125–128
Benckart, Ted, 122
Benham, Dan, 119–120
Bergman, Howard, 11–13
Bergman, Marsha, 13

Bergman, Mary, 136
Big Dandy, Texas, 109
Bloomington, Indiana, 122
Blue Ash, Ohio, 92
Bonneville, Utah, 162
Bossert, Muriel, 127–128
Bossert, Walter, 127–128
Boston, Massachusetts, 67, 161
Bradley University, 138
Braking system, 57, 156–157. See also
　121 brakes
Britton, Mary, 126–127
Britton, William, 126–127
Brockway trucks, 25
Buffalo, New York, 130
Building Model Trucks, 171
Bureau of Motor Carrier Safety, 79
Burger, Edward, 93–94
Byler, Ray, 71–75, 84, 86

C & H Transportation Company, 110
Cab, 38–43
Cab-over-engine, 14, 16, 17, 27, 37,
　40–42
Cab-under tractor, 177
Camper, 20
Careers, nondriving
　accounting, 149–150
　advertising, 138–139
　claims, 148–149
　clerical jobs, 144–145
　data processing, 149
　freight movement, 146–148
　insurance, 148–149
　maintenance and repair, 150–152
　management and administration,
　　136–139, 152–154
　rates and billing, 149
　safety, 148–149
　sales, 137–138, 145–146
　teaching, 134, 136–137
Cargo, unusual, 122–124
Carstensen Freight Lines, 106–107
Castorland, New York, 65
CB radio. See Citizens Band radio
Cedar Rapids, Iowa, 107
Cement mixer, 15
Chapman, Wallace, 93–94
Charging system, 44, 46

Chassis, 38, 44
Chatsworth, Ontario, 162
Chattanooga, Tennessee, 93–94
Chattanooga Glass Company, 93
Chevrolet trucks, 26, 52, 90
Chicago, Illinois, 81, 107, 138, 154,
　161
Chicago Academy of Fine Arts, 138
Children's Museum (Indianapolis), 123
Citizens Band radio, 65, 74, 93–95,
　97–105, 159, 164
Claims, 148–149
Claims adjuster. See Claims
Clark, Brant, 85
Cleveland, Ohio, 74, 145
Climax Manufacturing Company, 65–
　66, 68
Clinton, Iowa, 107
Co-drivers, 71, 82, 126–130
COE. See Cab-over-engine
Computerization, 135. See also Data
　processing
Consolidated Freightways, Inc., 108
Construction trucks, 15, 27
Conventional cabs, 28, 37, 40–42
　tilt-hood, 41
Conventions and exhibitions
　Big "I," The, 161
　Canadian Trucking Industry Trade
　　Show, 161
　International Trucking Show, 160–
　　161
　Mid-America Trucking Show, 161
　National Canadian Trucking Con-
　　vention and Exhibition, 161
　National Trucker's Convention, 161
　New England Truck and Truck
　　Equipment Show, 161
　Northeast Regional Trucker's Fair
　　and CB Jamboree, 161
　Truck Week, 80–81, 161
　Truckers Convention (Overdrive),
　　161
　Truckers Days, 161
　Truckers Jamboree and Expo, 161
Cooling system, 48–49
Cormorack, New York, 92
Costs, ownership, 84–85
C. R. England and Sons, 68–69

Crane Carrier Corporation trucks, 26, 172
Crankshaft, 48
Cranston, Rhode Island, 11
Crouch Freight Systems, 119
Cummins engine, 69, 162

Dallas, Texas, 154
Dana Corporation, 72
Data processing, 149
Datsun trucks, 14–15
Davenport, Iowa, 106
Dayton wheels, 73
Decker, Robert, 136
Delaney, Harold, 92
Delaware River, 122
Diamond Reo trucks, 26
Differential, 54–55
    tandem, 54
    twin-screw, 55
"Directory of Transportation Education," 145
Dispatcher, 69, 148. See also Freight movement
Dock worker. See Freight movement
Dolly, 19
"Doodlebug." See Dolly
Doubles, 18–19
Douglas, Charlie, 161, 165
Down time, 38
Drag races. See Racing, truck
Dragfoiler, 43
Drive train, 53–54
Driver, local, 61–65
Driver, long-distance, 65–75
Driver of the Month, 108
Driver of the Year, 108–110
    American Trucking Associations, Inc., 109–110
    Missouri, 110
    New York, 109
    Texas, 110
Driver preparation, 76–84
Drivers, women, 110–112, 125–133
Driving, relay, 68
Drops, 71
Dump trucks, 15, 63–64, 77
Dunham, Rodney W., 153

Dynamometer, 151–152. See also Troubleshooting

Eighteen wheeler, 11, 19, 73, 76
Electrical system, 44–46
Electrucks. See New York Telephone Company
Elementary Electronics, 99
Ellis, Wanda, 136–137
Elmwood, Kansas, 119
Employment outlook, 158
Engine, diesel, 49–53, 152. See also Cummins engine
Engine, four-cycle
    diesel, 50–52
    gasoline, 47–49, 51, 53
Engine, gas turbine, 53
Engine, gasoline, 44–49, 51, 53
Engine retarder, 58–59
Etter, James E., 171–172
"Extra board," 82

"Fifth wheel," 17, 19, 73
55 mph limit, imposition of, 97–98
"Fingerprinting," 71
Fire truck, 24
Flatbed trailer, 22
FMVSS 121 air brakes. See 121 brakes
Ford, Henry, 178
Ford Motor Company, 138–139, 145
Ford trucks, 17, 20, 41, 85
Ft. Washington, Pennsylvania, 176
Fort Wayne, Indiana, 71, 74
Fort Worth, Texas, 119–120
Foster, Neal, 106–108
Fox Valley Technical Institute (Wisconsin), 134, 136
Fram/Autolite Corporation, 111
Freight movement, 146–148
Freightliner trucks, 16, 27
"Fuel squeezers," 51–52
Fuel system, diesel, 50
FWD trucks, 27

Garbage trucks, 15, 22, 26
Gazda, Lisa, 128–129
Gazda, Richard, 128–129
Glad hands, 73, 133
GMC trucks, 22, 28, 37, 43, 66

Gold-leafing, 142
Grant, J. B., 152
Gray, Elizabeth "Liz," 138–139
Greenville, Ohio, 68
Gypo, 132

Haessner Publishing Company, 171
Hall, Julie, 128–129
HART, 99
Hatch, Roger James, 121
Hayes, Kenneth, 130–131
Hayes, Muriel, 130–131
Hendrickson Manufacturing Company, 176
Hendrickson trucks, 28
High Springs, Florida, 94
Hobbies, trucking
    Citizens Band radio, 164
    games, 165–166
    radio, 165
    scale models, 167–171
        American Industrial Models, 171
        AMT, 167, 169
        Big Rigs, 167, 169
        Ertl, 167–168, 171
        Lindberg, 171
Hollywood, Alabama, 123
Hopkinton, Rhode Island, 11

Ignition system, 45
Incentives, trucking, 106–124
Indianapolis, Indiana, 74, 118, 123, 143, 153
Indianapolis Raceway Park, 161
Instrument panel, 39
Insurance, 148–149
Insurance officer. See Insurance
International Harvester Company
    Fort Worth Sales and Service Center, 121
    McArdle International, 122
    Northside International, 137–138
    Regional Truck Training Centers, 154–157
    Transtar Rose American Road Show, 163
    Truck Division, 154, 163
    Truck Engine Plant, 143

Used Truck Center, Melrose Park, Illinois, 85
International trucks, 23, 28, 39, 41, 107, 120, 122, 137–138, 146, 152, 168
Interstate Commerce Commission, 67, 73, 125–126
Irvin, David, 87
Irvin, Gregg, 63–65
Irvin, Roland, 68–71

Jackknife, 58
Jake Brake. See Engine retarder
Jake"er." See Engine retarder
James, Larry, 165
Jargon, truckers', 97–105
Jensen, Phil, 171
Jernigan, Linda Jean, 111
Jobs, finding, 82
John, Donna, 131–132, 134
Johnson, W. W., 153
Joseph Chiappone Lime Spreading, 134

K & M Enterprises, 131
Keehan, W. E., 153
Kenworth trucks, 19–20, 29, 68, 71, 162
Kilpatrick, William, 116
Kingpin, 17
Kingsport, Tennessee, 74
Kinkle, James, 162
Knights of the Road, 91–96, 100, 110
Kroack, Lou, 171
K-Whopper. See Kenworth trucks

Labor, Department of, 158
Lamm, Michael, 173
Landing gear, 17, 19
Langlinais, Kenneth, 92–93
Leutze, Emmanuel, 122
Lexington, Illinois, 161
Log book, 70, 73, 87
Log sheet. See Log book
Lone Star Big Rig Truck Race and Roadeo Championship, 162
Long Island, New York, 130
Los Angeles, California, 125

MacDonald, Bernice, 134, 136–137
Mack trucks, 14–15, 29, 34–35, 37,
  65, 71, 73–74, 77, 83, 123, 132,
  142, 168
Mack Trucks, Inc., 137–139, 166
Magazines, trucking
  Heavy Duty Trucking, 167, 176
  Open Road, 78, 110, 112, 116, 130,
  138
  Overdrive, 84, 161, 171
  Owner Operator, 86, 167, 171, 174
  Traffic World, 112
Maintenance and repair, 150–152
Maintenance Man of the Year, 112
Mallicoat, Ronald, 107
Malone, Jerry "Tyrone," 162
Marmon trucks, 29
Mason and Dixon Lines, Inc., 71, 74,
  84
McArdle, Robert, 122
McLean, William D., 84
Mead, Albert L., 108–109
Mechanics, truck. See Maintenance
  and repair
Medals
  Carnegie Medal, 93
  Presidential Medal of Honor for
  Lifesaving on the Highways, 10
Medford, Oregon, 108
Melvin Strickland Company, 129
Milesburg, Pennsylvania, 68–69
Miller, Frank, 121
Million Mile Award, 137
Milton Bradley Company, 166
Minneapolis, Minnesota, 121
Mitchell Transport Company, 112
Model trucks, 167–170
Modelers, 171–172
Moon Freight Lines, 122
Motor Vehicle Manufacturers Asso-
  ciation, 84
Motorcar Transport Company, 112
Mount Airy, North Carolina, 129
Movies, trucking, 165
Muthler, Richard, 77
Myers, Robert, 112

Napier, Chuck, 165
NASA, 176

National Association of Trade and
  Technical Schools (NATTS), 79
National Automobile Transportation
  Association, 112
National Institute for Automotive Ex-
  cellence, 152
Nelson, Bonnie, 162–163
New London, Connecticut, 11
New Orleans, Louisiana, 161
New York, New York, 67, 130, 176
New York Telephone Company, 176
916 Area Vocational Technical Insti-
  tute (Minnesota), 80–81
Northampton, Massachusetts, 163
Nottoli, Jerry, 138

O'Brien, Mike, 85
Off-road applications, 15, 35, 56
  logging, 35
  Mack-Pack, 35
Oil filter system, 50
121 brakes, 59, 156–157
Ontario, California, 162
Ontario Motor Speedway, 162
Oshkosh trucks, 25
Osterland, Inc., 26
Owner-operators, 74, 84–90, 107, 111

Pacific "Roughneck" truck, 30
Parker Brothers, 166
Parkhill Truck Company, 108
"Pete." See Peterbilt trucks
Peterbilt trucks, 30, 78, 161
Pickup trucks, 14–15, 20
Pontiac, Michigan, 112
Popular Mechanics, 116, 173
Power divider, 56
Preston, B. W., 82
Pre-trip inspection, 70, 72–73
Preventative maintenance, 86, 150–
  151
Providence, Rhode Island, 11, 67–68,
  108
Puggle, Paul, 95–96
Pump jockey, 78
Purdum, Cassandra "Sandi," 111–112

Queen of the Road, 110–112

Racing, truck, 161–163
Radio stations, truckers', 111, 161, 165
Ramsey, Wayne, 92–93
REACT, 99–100
Reading, Pennsylvania, 71
Recreational activities, truckers', 159–172
Reimers, T. E., 153
Reno, Jack, 165
Rescue vehicle (crash fire), 30
Reuben Wells, the, 123
Rhode Island Truck Owners Association, 13
Rich, Charlie, 160–161
Richmond, Indiana, 153
River Grove, Illinois, 81
Roadeo, 112–121
  qualifications, 113
  nondriving tests, 113
  skills tests, 114–116
Rochester, New York, 130
Rock Island, Illinois, 107
Ross, Robert, 153
Ryder tractor, 176

Sacramento, California, 111
Safety, 148–149
Safety director. See Safety
St. Lawrence Freightways, 130
Salt Lake City, Utah, 69
San Diego, California, 128
San Leandro, California, 154
Sanitation vehicles, 15, 22, 26
Schools, truck driving, 79–82, 134
Seattle, Washington, 123
Semi-trailers, 17, 44, 76
  Budd, 17, 33
  Dorsey AirFlect, 32
  lowboy (gooseneck), 34
  "possum belly," 33
  Trailmobile platform, 32
  van, 14, 32
  vehicle carriers, 34
  See also Trailers
Shinoda, Larry, 174, 178
Showker, Inc., 166
Shugart, Dan R., 108
Shutdown, truckers', 98

Simeral, Lesley, 137, 145
Sleepers, 17, 19–20, 37, 123
Snowplow, 25
Snyder, William, 162
Songs, trucking, 164
Sparkplugs. See Ignition system
Spong, Alfred, 112
Springfield, Vermont, 131
Stake body truck, 22
Statewide Towing Association of Massachusetts, 163
Steinhoek, Harley, 95–96
Sterling, Illinois, 107
Straight trucks, 15, 20
Strick, Inc., 176–177
Sullivan, Chuck, 165
Sun Oil Company, 11
Super Boss. See Malone, Jerry "Tyrone"
Superstar Athletic Competition, 110–111
Syracuse, New York, 61

Tandem, 15, 54, 123
Tank truck, 33
Terminal manager. See Freight movement
Testor Corporation, 169
Texas State Technical Institute, 82
Thermo King, 33, 162
Tonawanda, New York, 108
Tow trucks, 24
Tractors, 16–17
Tracy, Donna, 84
Trailers, 15–19. See also Semi-trailers
Transit mixers, 22
Transmission, 53–56, 126
  automatic vs. manual, 56
  Road Ranger, 69
  Spicer 50 Series, 55
Transportation, Department of, 76, 154
"Transtar Rose." See Nelson, Bonnie
Triples, 18–19
Tri-State Motor Transit Company, 108
Triton College, 81
Troubleshooting, 155. See also Dynamometer
Truck assembly, 135, 141–143

Truck Drivers' Country Music Awards, 160–161
Truck Drivers Dictionary and Glossary, 100
Truck stop, 77–78
Trucks, kinds of
  camper, 20
  construction, 15, 27
  dump, 15, 63–64, 77
  flatbed, 22
  fire, 24
  garbage (sanitation), 15, 22, 26
  pickup, 14–15, 20
  rescue, 30
  snowplow, 25
  stake body, 22
  straight, 15, 20
  tank, 33
  tow, 24
  transit mixer, 22
  wrecker, 15
Tuscaloosa, Alabama, 93

Underwood Transfer Company, Inc., 123

Van (truck), 21
Vecchio, Karen, 132, 134,
Volvo trucks, 31
Vortex, 42–43. *See also* Wind deflector

Walker, Wylie B., 93
Walkersville, Maryland, 111
Walter Motor Truck Company, 30
Walter Rapid Intervention vehicle, 30
Washington Crossing, Pennsylvania, 122
"Washington Crossing the Delaware," 122
Washington, D.C., 152
Waters, Lee, 125, 126
Watertown, New York, 61, 130, 134
Webster City, Iowa, 95
Welk, Olen "Oley," 109–110
Westcott, Eunice, 62
Westcott, Norman, 61–62
Wheeling, West Virginia, 161
White Bear Lake, Minnesota, 81
White Motor Corporation, 25, 43
White trucks, 16, 23, 31, 33, 88
Wilcox, Charles A., Jr., 130
William K. Walthers, Inc., 169–170
Wind deflector, 43, 69, 173. *See also* Aerodynamics
Wind resistance, 17, 42–43. *See also* Aerodynamics
Wisconsin Motor Carriers Association, 137
Wisconsin Transportation Company, 137
Woodsboro, Maryland, 112
Wrangler, 78
Wreckers, 15

ABOUT THE AUTHOR

Hope Irvin Marston's interest in trucks and trucking was prompted by the seven professional truckers in her family. "They made trucking sound so exciting. I began to read trucking magazines to learn more. I would have read books if I could have found any," she says. "My students kept asking for a book on the big rigs, so I decided to write one myself."

Mrs. Marston is a junior high school librarian in Watertown, New York. She resides with her husband, three boxers, a cocker spaniel, and a St. Bernard in nearby Black River. A native of central Pennsylvania, she began her writing career as a stringer for the *Lewiston* (Maine) *Sun*. Her book is based on personal conversations with truckers, her extensive reading, and tours of the Mack plants in Allentown and Macungie, Pennsylvania.

388.302
MAR   Marston, Hope Irvin

             Trucks, trucking,
             and you

DATE DUE			
OCT 26 81			
JAN 3 '82			
OCT00			
OCT 14			